Effective Instruction

Tamar Levin with Ruth Long

The Association for Supervision and Curriculum Development
225 North Washington Street   Alexandria, Virginia 22314

Editing:
Ronald S. Brandt, ASCD Executive Editor
Nancy Carter Modrak, Assistant Editor

Cover Design: Great, Incorporated

Stock Number: 611-80212
Library of Congress Catalog Card Number: 80-70793
ISBN 0-87120-105-4

Contents

Foreword

This is an exciting book. Exciting because it speaks to that age-old request that permeates every school in America and every room where teachers gather: "Help me to be a better teacher."

All too often, the books designed to minister to that deep-felt need of teachers are full of jargon, unresearched concepts, and theories that teachers tell us look magnificent from behind a professor's desk, but which fail miserably in the marketplace—the classroom. All too often those same books are written in an obtuse, obfuscated style that finds the teacher throwing up his or her hands in horror after reading only a few pages. If we might paraphrase Winston Churchill, it is probably true in education that so very much is written by so very many to be read by so very few. It is one of the tragedies of this profession that, while charged with being the prime communicators in our society we seldom come near living up to what is expected of us.

Tamar Levin has compiled a book dealing with the classroom variables which, research throughout the world has shown, have the most telling impact on learning. She and Ruth Long report these studies in a clear, concise, prose which cuts through to the heart of the research and isolates the essential qualities for the reader. Teachers searching for new ideas to help their own teaching will learn, for example, that research shows that students who are more involved in the learning process invariably take seats near the teacher. The simple task of changing seating assignments periodically may help expand the circle of active learners in a given classroom. Teachers may also recognize themselves as the authors describe how students react if they realize they may be called on to answer a question as opposed to their actions if they are reasonably sure they will not be singled out that particular day. It is interesting that this exact situation has been the subject of a nationally-syndicated comic strip recently. That comic strip had the student, who was unprepared to answer questions on the day's lesson, outwitting the teacher by constantly raising his hand as if thoroughly prepared.

Teachers may also recognize themselves as guilty of providing instructional cues to only a few members of their class, thereby effectively shutting out other class members because the selected group is not a true cross section of the total class.

The book discusses evaluation instruments that have been used for self-evaluation, for student evaluation, and for evaluation of class atmosphere. The authors make the point that increasingly evaluation instruments are being used to provide feedback for improvement rather than as a process of passive judgment, another factor teachers will appreciate.

The annotated bibliography may prove to be one of the most popular sections. It includes articles which emphasize the feasibility of implementing the particular ideas that are suggested in the book. Summarized, the articles describe how students were tested, the conditions under which the tests were given, and the results that were obtained.

Individual teachers—perhaps individual faculties—will greatly benefit from this book. It would be exciting to have a faculty study the book, pick from it several ideas, discuss them, and implement them in an individual school.

ASCD has published some important books over the years. This is another such offering.

BARBARA DAY
President, 1980-81
Association for Supervision and
Curriculum Development

Preface

This book has grown out of a special project of the International Association for the Evaluation of Educational Achievement (IEA). This worldwide organization has, for the past two decades, carried out large international studies to determine the effects of home, school, teachers, instruction, and the curriculum on the cognitive and affective outcomes of student learning in different school subjects. It was evident in all these studies that the *interaction between teachers and students* in the classroom was the major factor in accounting for the cognitive learning of the students, their interest in the school subjects and school learning, and their confidence in their own learning capabilities.

At the request of most of the participating countries, IEA agreed to sponsor an international study of the factors in the classroom which are most important for the improvement of student achievement, interests, and attitudes. The major concern of the countries was to identify and study those classroom processes which have been responsible for the major learning differences among students within a classroom, which account for the differences in student achievement among the classrooms in a nation, as well as the achievement differences between the nations. The national representatives in the IEA were especially interested in those classroom processes which could be readily used by a teacher and which could clearly be demonstrated to improve the learning of most of the students in as short a period of time as three months.

Dr. Tamar Levin, of the School of Education of Tel Aviv University, was appointed as the International Coordinator for this classroom learning study. She and her assistants developed the overall plan for the study which will involve classrooms in about 15 nations. She also prepared a lengthy detailed report in which she reviewed the research findings throughout the world on the classroom variables and processes which have the greatest effects on learning in each of the countries. It is evident that a small number of these variables and processes have almost equally great effects on learning in each of the countries where they have been studied.

As a member of the International Advisory Committee for this study, I was much impressed by the clarity of the evidence on these variables. I urged Dr. Levin to write a shorter book which would enable teachers throughout the world to learn about these very effective variables and processes and to help them explore the use of these variables in their own classrooms. She has done a skillful writing job in which she explains each of the processes, indicates why they are so important, and summarizes the evidence on the effectiveness of the processes on student learning. She also offers suggestions to teachers to help them explore the use of these processes in their own classrooms.

However, no matter how skillfully she has presented the case for each of these processes, they are still only inert ideas on paper. They can come to life with their full potentiality only when they are adapted to the needs of each classroom by the teacher and then actually used with the students in the class. It is my hope that all readers of this book will be inspired to try these processes in their own classrooms for even as short a period as a few weeks.

But I doubt that solitary readers of this book can, on their own, make full use of these ideas. What is likely to be very effective is an informal trio or quartet of teachers who meet on their own a few times to read and discuss the ideas in this book. Such a trio or quartet ideally should be composed of teacher friends. It might even include teachers who teach at different levels of education from the kindergarten to the graduate and professional schools.

These teachers should try to determine the extent to which they already use these processes in their classrooms. Then they should discuss some of their highly successful as well as unsuccessful classroom instances (or students) to determine whether these processes can explain both the positive and negative examples in their own classrooms. If the discussion has gone this far, the teachers should attempt to use these processes for a few sessions in their own classes. If these prove to be positive, the teachers should then attempt to use them for an entire quarter or semester, observing very carefully some of the effects they have on the improvement of learning, interests, and attitudes of each of their students.

BENJAMIN S. BLOOM
Distinguished Service Professor
of Education
University of Chicago

Introduction

A small number of instructional and learning processes have consistently made major improvements in the learning of most students in a class or school. The major purpose of this book is to share these findings with those who are responsible for educating students, whether they are curriculum developers, supervisors, administrators, policy makers, educational researchers, or teachers. If teachers can adapt these ideas to their own classrooms, student achievement should improve significantly.

The book focuses on three types of variables in classroom learning and instruction: (1) *active learning time,* (2) *feedback and corrective procedures,* and (3) *instructional cues.* Strong research evidence led us to recognize the powerful effects of these variables in determining school learning. Each variable makes a unique contribution to the quality of the process and outcomes of learning. They also share three characteristics. First, they are highly related to student learning outcomes. Second, they are alterable, and their effects can be observed within a relatively short time. Third, the variables can be used effectively by teachers at any level of education and in any subject area.

We describe the nature of each of the variables and the conditions under which they are likely to determine successful learning for most students in a class. We also explain why these variables have such powerful effects on learning and how a teacher can use them in many different ways to improve instruction and learning. These ideas and procedures allow freedom for each teacher to select and develop a variety of techniques for managing effective learning in the classroom. But they can be effective only if teachers understand them and adapt them to the needs of their students.

If the teacher is successful in implementing one or more of these processes, there should be noticeable differences in students (increased achievement, positive attitudes, greater interest in and motivation for learning) within a relatively short period. Teachers will also notice their own increased satisfaction, self-confidence, and enthusiasm about teaching.

There are, of course, other variables and processes that affect learning and instruction, but in this book we discuss the few variables and processes that are believed to produce the *greatest* effects.

1. Active Learning Time

Students differ in the degree to which they actively learn. Some students spend most of their time in class actively involved while others spend much of the time daydreaming, looking out the window, or involved in activities unrelated to learning. An observer can translate these actions into estimates of the percent of time each student is actively engaged in classroom learning, which is an index of the degree of the student's involvement in learning. Although students may spend equal amounts of time in class, they vary greatly in their involvement (Boydell, 1975; Dennison, 1976; Fibly and others, 1977; Gump, 1971).

The degree of such involvement, however, is not always easily observable. A student may take appropriate notes, carry out written exercises, and express interest. This participation is overt and observable. It is possible for another student to be equally involved and highly interested, yet in a manner that is covert and not easily observed. This second student follows the teacher's explanations, relates them to what he or she already knows, and figures out solutions to particular exercises. Overt (observable) and covert (unobservable) types of involvement in learning both manifest active learning. Ideally, the amount of time a student is actively engaged in learning should be determined by the degree of both covert and overt involvement.

Teachers are aware that active involvement in classroom learning is necessary for effective learning and achieving desired outcomes. They expect students who are highly involved in learning activities, who spend more time learning in the classroom, to do well on tests, have more interest in the subject, and have a positive view of themselves in relation to learning. In contrast, they expect students who spend little time in classroom learning to do poorly on tests, have little interest in school, and have a negative view about themselves, especially as learners.

Active learning time as a measure of student involvement in class has

1

long been considered by educators and researchers to be central and vital to instruction. As early as 1884, Currie believed:

> The art of teaching . . . comprehends all the means by which a teacher sustains the attention of his class. By attention we do not mean the mere absence of noise . . . or that inert passive state in which the class . . . gives no symptom of mental life. . . . The only satisfactory attention is that which is given voluntarily and steadily by all during the entire instruction, and in which the mental attitude of the class is actively engaged along with the teacher in working out their own instruction.

Almost a hundred years later, in searching for promising directions to improve educational achievement, the 1978 report of the National Academy of Education stressed that "the answer to the question of how schools can improve educational attainment lies in spending more time on those attainments we value. There is a striking convergence of evidence that points to the role of time-on-task—"engaged time"—in improving performance in school subject matters."

The Relationship Between Active Learning Time and Achievement

One way of studying the relationship between the degree of students' active involvement in learning and their achievement is to observe selected groups of students in one classroom—students the teacher identifies as good or poor achievers—and examine the differences in their degree of involvement. Then it is also possible to compare their degree of involvement to their achievement. Studies that have used either one of these approaches (Good and Beckerman, 1978; Perkins, 1965) generally demonstrate that, within a classroom, *students who are more involved in their learning have higher achievement than students who are less involved in classroom learning activities.*

For example, high and low achieving students were observed working on their own, in study groups, and studying under the guidance of their teacher (Levin and others, 1980). While high achievers were actively involved in learning for 70 percent of the time, students who were identified as low achievers were actively involved in learning only 50 percent of the time. Williams (1970) identified students as "participants," "intermediate participants," or "nonparticipants" based on their amount of overt participation in class. When these groups were compared in terms of achievement, Williams found significant differences among them.

Numerous studies have used an overt measure of student involvement (Attwell and others, 1967; Berliner, 1979; Cobb, 1970, 1972; Edminston and Rhoades, 1959; Gaver and Richards, 1979; Lahaderne, 1968; Morsh,

1956; Olson, 1931; Samuels and Turnure, 1974; Stallings, 1976; Stallings and Kaskowitz, 1974; Turnure and Samuels, 1972). They typically found a correlation between student involvement and achievement.

Other studies have used covert measures of student involvement (Krauskopf, 1963; Siegel and others, 1963) or both overt and covert measures of involvement (Hudgins, 1966; Özcelik, 1973). The covert measure, based on the stimulated recall technique developed by Bloom (1953) requires students to recall the thoughts they had at various critical points during a class session. Their responses then are classified as either relevant or irrelevant to the learning.

For example, Siegel and others (1963) studied the relationship of college students' relevant thinking to their achievement. Students were recorded on video tape while listening to a 20-minute lecture. A correlation was found between the degree of relevant thinking and the items that tested students' understanding of the major ideas presented during the lecture. In contrast, no correlation was found between their relevant thinking and the test items that reflected knowledge they acquired outside the classroom. The discrepancy between the correlations indicates that a covert measure of student involvement in classroom instruction is indeed a good predictor of student success in the learning that takes place in the classroom.

Other research focuses on the relationship between the average degree of participation in *different* classes and their mean performance levels. These relationships are established *between* classrooms. Within a class, those students who spend more time on active learning attain higher levels of achievement than do students who spend less time involved in the learning. Likewise, classes in which students spend more time involved in learning achieve higher levels of performance than classes in which students spend less time actually involved in learning. It is evident that more active learning time results in greater learning.

Variability in Active Learning Time

Differences in degree of involvement are highly related to student characteristics. Typically, aptitude or intelligence scores measure cognitive characteristics of students, while motivation, self-esteem, or confidence measure students' affective characteristics. Williams James (1890) made one of the earliest attempts to explain the great variation in participation. He identified student interest as the chief determinant influencing the degree of active learning. Recent studies demonstrate the correlation between such affective measures as self-concept or attitudes toward schools and student involvement (Anderson, 1973; Özcelik, 1973; Block, 1970;

Lahaderne, 1968; Hecht, 1977). In the past, such evidence was taken as an indication that active student learning time is determined by unalterable student characteristics. If such stable characteristics as intelligence or aptitude scores do determine students' degree of involvement, then there is little that schools and teachers can do to increase active learning time.

But every teacher knows that in real classroom situations students who are most involved in learning are not always those with high aptitude scores, nor are students who are less involved always the ones with lower scores. Other student characteristics may be more important in determining the degree of involvement.

In his model of school learning, Carroll (1963) defined active learning time as the central variable in school learning and differentiated between time allowed for students to learn *(elapsed time)* and time students are actually involved in learning *(active learning time)*. Carroll hypothesized that if each student is allowed to spend the time needed to learn something to a predetermined criterion, then the student should be able to attain the required level of achievement, provided that he or she uses that time. Conversely, if a student is not allowed enough time or does not spend the required time, then he or she would most probably fail to attain the desired level of achievement. Carroll essentially proposed that the degree of school learning is determined by the amount of time the student actually spends in learning relative to the time he or she needs to spend.

In contrast, Bloom (1968) conceptualized students' involvement in learning as a function of their relevant affective and cognitive characteristics. These are the prerequisite skills and knowledge that the student needs to possess before learning a specific new task. The relevant affective characteristics are motivation for learning, attitudes toward school, and the student's self-concept as a learner (Anderson, 1973; Block, 1970; Özcelik, 1973; Hecht, 1977). Research suggests two conditions under which we can *increase* the degree of student involvement in learning: first, instructional processes should evoke those activities of the student that are relevant to the learning task and, second, the student should be motivated to learn and possess the appropriate prerequisites needed to learn a particular task.

The Effects of Instructional Conditions on Involvement

Several studies have examined whether active learning time or student involvement in learning can be altered by particular instructional techniques or processes. Most of the studies were carried out under conditions similar to regular classroom situations and examined a different aspect of the instructional learning processes.

Two of the earliest experimental studies in this area were by Van Wagenen and Travers (1963) and by Travers and others (1964). In the Van Wagenen and Travers study, the teacher taught German vocabulary to fourth, fifth, or sixth-graders for three consecutive days. Only half the students were called on in class. These students learned by recitation and were verbally reinforced for their responses. The other half were able to observe only the cards and performance of the students who interacted with the teacher and the materials.

Each day of the experiment the two groups were given an achievement test. The participant students performed better than the nonparticipant students; moreover, the difference in achievement between the two groups increased from the first to the third day of the experiment. In this study, direct interaction with the learning materials and the teacher produced higher levels of achievement than merely listening to or watching the interaction.

Vohs (1964) constructed learning situations that were intended to *decrease* the amount and quality of student involvement. Four study groups were required to listen to a speech. During the speech one group of students listened without being distracted; a second group was instructed to draw a line through every letter "e" in a textbook; a third group carried out specific instructions to draw rows of geometric figures; and the fourth group did simple arithmetic operations. The group of students who listened to the speech without distractions had higher achievement over the content of the speech than had the other groups. Each succeeding distraction decreased the amount and quality of time spent listening to the speech.

Carroll and Spearitt (1967) studied whether the quality of instructional materials affects the degree of student involvement in learning. They used two sets of instructional materials. One emphasized a high quality of instructional information. A new language rule was presented to the students, who were tested before the next rule was presented. When they made mistakes, they returned to the page on which the rules were fully explained. The learning materials were clear and organized. In contrast, the second set of instructional materials provided too much information at one time and in a disorganized manner. When students made errors they referred to explanations that were inadequate. When the instructional materials were clear and organized, students were more likely to be actively involved in their learning. They tended to lose interest and to spend less time actively involved in learning when the instructional materials were unclear.

Several researchers studied the effects of particular types of instructional settings on the degree of student involvement in learning (Good and Beckerman, 1978; Kounine and Gump, 1974; McDonald, 1976; Anderson and Scott, 1978; Stallings and Kaskowitz, 1974). In general, these studies indicate that some instructional settings tend to minimize involvement for the majority of students. In particular, small study groups without adult supervision produce very low levels of student involvement in learning, but group discussions supervised by teachers produce a higher degree of involvement.

Reinforcement can also increase individual students' participation in group learning situations (Bushnell and others, 1968; Chadwick and Day, 1971; Hops and Cobb, 1972; Packard, 1970; Walker and others, 1969). Ferritor and others (1972) were able to increase the amount of time students were actively involved by reinforcing them for being on task and doing arithmetic problems correctly. Although researchers differ greatly in their approaches, they all indicate that student involvement can be significantly altered. They demonstrate that selectively providing or depriving students of certain conditions can directly increase or decrease the active learning time of individual students or the level of involvement of the entire class.

All the studies share one underlying principle. If instructional processes and procedures *elicit* student behavior relevant to the learning task, student involvement is likely to increase. In contrast, if the instructional conditions shift student attention from the main foci of the learning task, or if the instruction is misleading or disturbing, then active learning time is likely to decrease to a substantial degree. Thus, instructional conditions as well as explanations and directions for learning have the potential to alter student involvement in learning.

The Effects of Preparation on Involvement

Student involvement depends also on some of the characteristics that students bring to a learning situation. For instance, if we were required to sit in a class and learn complex new subject matter without adequate prior preparation, we might have great difficulty learning the subject matter, regardless of how good the instruction is. And, most likely, we would find it difficult to become actively involved in the class.

Each new learning task requires some cognitive prerequisites on the part of the student. These prerequisites help students relate new ideas, skills, or procedures to what they already know, and better understand the instruction.

In the past, research emphasized the differences between fast and slow students (Ellson and others, 1965; Lloyd, 1971; Sheppard and Mac-Dermot, 1970; Shimron, 1976; Steg and others, 1968; Zeaman and House,

1963, 1967). In general, the findings demonstrate that slow learners take much more time to get started on learning activities than do faster learners. Zeaman and House (1963) stressed that "the difference between fast and slow learners is not so much the rate at which improvement takes place, once it starts, but rather the number of trials for learning to start" (p. 162).

What are the differences between groups of students that enable one group to get involved immediately in the learning while the other .group delays? Will simply providing more time help slow students participate actively in learning? How can we decrease procrastination as instruction begins?

Most of the studies on the relationship between student characteristics and student involvement were carried out within the framework of the mastery learning strategy. They typically involve a group of students learning certain materials organized in a series of units or chapters in a text; students are expected to achieve a preset performance level at the end of each learning unit. Students who do not attain the predetermined mastery level are usually given additional time and help in the form of alternate learning materials, small-group study, peer tutoring, and so forth. Then they are tested again to determine whether the additional time and learning helped them reach the preset performance standard. Under the usual conditions of group instruction, the group as a whole moves to the next learning unit after the majority of students has attained mastery over the previous unit or chapter. Similar procedures are employed for each learning unit in the series. Ideally, most of the corrective work is done outside of class time.

The mastery learning studies show that when students are given extra time and appropriate help, and when they are motivated to learn, 80 percent or more can finally attain the preset mastery level on each learning unit. One of the more striking and consistent results of these studies is the pattern of learning of mastery groups versus control groups (Anderson, 1973, 1976; Arlin, 1973; Block, 1970; Levin, 1975; Özcelik, 1973). Control and mastery groups start at the same achievement level. As learning progresses, it is apparent that the mean performance level of the mastery groups becomes significantly higher than that of the control groups. This is true even before the mastery students engage in the corrective process.

The control and mastery groups have similar group instruction and use the same learning materials. The only difference is that the students in the mastery group are provided additional time and help to correct their learning difficulties, while the control group is not given such help. Even though both groups are similarly involved in learning on the first unit or chapter, as learning progresses from unit to unit, student involvement increases in the mastery group and decreases in the control group.

In the study by Anderson (1973, 1976), for example, the mastery and control groups spent about the same percent of time on task in class during the first learning unit (74 and 76 percent, respectively). During the second unit, the mastery group was involved 78 percent of the time, while the control group spent only 64 percent of the time in active learning. By the third unit, the students in the mastery group were, on the average, involved in active learning 82 percent of the time compared to only 62 percent of the time for the average student in the control group.

These results suggest several explanations. First, the students in the mastery group are provided with the cognitive prerequisites necessary for each new learning unit in the series. Bloom (1976) calls them cognitive entry behaviors. Students who acquire the necessary prerequisites are better able to understand the instruction and, as a result, become more involved in the learning. Second, students in the mastery group develop higher levels of motivation for later units in the series. Since they have experienced success in the earlier units, they are more confident in their ability to learn well and to succeed in subsequent units. Students in the mastery group seem more able to make good use of the learning time available in class. In contrast, many students in the control group are not likely to learn the subject. This would explain why their degree of active learning time decreases over a series of learning units.

Hecht (1977) presents strong evidence on the role of cognitive prerequisites in determining students' degree of involvement. Hecht used tenth-grade mastery and control groups to demonstrate that students who possess the prerequisites become involved in classroom learning. Students who reached the mastery standard, whether they learned under the mastery learning or control conditions, became equally involved in classroom learning. Students who did not acquire the necessary prerequisites, no matter what method of instruction was used, spent significantly less active learning time on the next unit. Students who did acquire the necessary prerequisites performed much higher on the final achievement test than did the students who had not acquired the appropriate prerequisites. Under mastery conditions, more students acquire the prerequisites and are involved in their learning.

Thus, when two groups of students begin with similar levels of performance and involvement in learning, they can become very different in both dimensions in a short period of time. The difference between the instructional conditions provided to these two groups is the additional time and corrective help that students in the mastery group receive to supplement their group instruction. This time is used to help the students correct mistakes and achieve the preset mastery standard. These processes and procedures are referred to as *feedback-corrective procedures*.

Implications for Classroom Practices

Changes in the degree of student involvement result in changes in student learning outcomes. Greater student involvement results in increased student achievement and other positive learning outcomes; decreases in the amount of engaged learning result in decreased student achievement and other learning outcomes. Student involvement is a strong determinant of learning outcomes, as illustrated in Figure 1.

Figure 1. The Relation of Student Characteristics and Instructional Processes to Student Involvement in Learning and Learning Outcomes

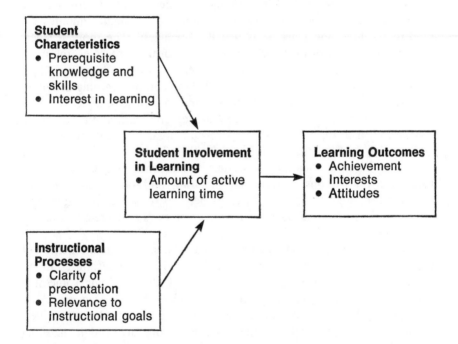

Figure 1 also shows that student involvement is largely affected by two sets of conditions—the appropriateness of instructional processes and procedures and the degree to which students are prepared to learn a new task. When instructional processes evoke student activities appropriate to the goals of learning, student involvement is likely to increase. Students who are better prepared for a new learning task will be more involved in learning than those who are less well prepared.

How to Improve Class Involvement

1. Devote more time to teaching-learning activities. Teachers who analyze their own instructional patterns become more aware of certain activities that do not contribute directly to either instruction or learning (such as recording student attendance, distributing materials, solving classroom organizational problems, or dealing with discipline problems). Activities that are essential to instruction include explaining, directing, probing, testing, listening to responses, and demonstrating new ideas and procedures. Several studies suggest that many teachers spend only a small part of each school day actually teaching (Alschuler and others, 1975; Conant, 1973; Cusick, 1973).

Teachers' activities can also be translated into estimates of time. Since only a fixed amount of time is available, its effective use is crucial. If a typical classroom session lasts about 50 minutes, the actual minutes devoted to teaching and learning is usually much less. The more teachers increase the amount of time for teaching and learning processes, the more opportunities students have to become actively involved in learning. Alternately, when much time is spent on nonteaching and nonlearning activities, students have less time and opportunity for involved learning.

There are many ways to increase teaching and learning time during a class period. The teacher could prepare and organize plans, procedures, and materials before instruction begins, rather than in class. The teacher could also distribute learning materials to students' desks, or prepare blackboard illustrations, audiovisual material, and other teaching aids ahead of class time. Essentially, teachers need to "observe" how they currently use class time and consider a variety of ways to increase teaching-learning time.

2. Increase active student participation. The most common method of maximizing student participation is eliciting their active responses to instruction. Active participation means that students are doing something with the learning materials or directions provided by the teacher. These activities can be observable or nonobservable. Students who write their responses or respond orally to questions are more involved in learning than students who listen, watch other students, or wait for the teacher to give further instructions.

Two-way communication between students and teachers or between students and learning materials is usually more effective than discussions among classmates without the guidance of an adult. Students seated near the teacher tend to be more involved in two-way communication than students seated further from the teacher (Kim and others, 1974). Jackson (1968) suggests that teachers can improve two-way communication and increase student involvement by moving about the classroom frequently and changing seating arrangements.

Many teachers establish a defined pattern of techniques for evoking overt student involvement. If teachers call on students in a predictable pattern, students will be actively engaged only when they expect to be called on. Ideally, they should be actively involved in learning even when other students are contributing to the class. Most are anxious to receive the teachers' approval as much as possible. They'll make a great effort to predict the questions they will be asked, when they will be expected to answer, and when the teacher will summarize the major points to be remembered. Under these conditions, some students become involved in their learning only when they believe it is necessary. If teachers usually repeat the major ideas at the beginning or end of the session, or in other ways indicate important (or less important) points, a number of students will become highly involved in learning only when the teacher signals what is important.

Changing patterns or techniques may be helpful. Instead of using fixed patterns to review or summarize the main ideas of a lesson, teachers should signal *frequently* to the students that *much* of what is discussed in class is important.

A class is not merely a group of 20 or 30 isolated individuals—it is a small social system in which students have much in common. The class as a whole can develop anxieties, a special climate, or pride, desires, and interests. Group reinforcement of student involvement or participation is effective in increasing participation. But some teachers too frequently reinforce only a small number of students (Brophy and Good, 1974). They need to reinforce as many students in the class as possible. The teacher also needs to find a great variety of ways to reinforce and reward both active learning and learning outcomes. A teacher is more likely to succeed in this by knowing students well enough to determine the interests, desires, and rewards they will respond to.

3. Make fluid transitions between activities. A classroom is a busy place in which many activities may occur simultaneously: students read aloud, talk, take notes, solve problems, listen, and so on. Sometimes several instructional settings are used during a single lesson—small groups, large groups, or individual desk work. In a typical classroom more than one concept, rule, or idea is discussed in a lesson. The transitions from one activity to another, from one setting to the next, all decrease student involvement in learning. Clearly, transitions are necessary, but the less time spent in transitions, the more students learn (Anderson and others, 1979).

Teachers must seek effective and efficient ways to make these transitions almost automatic and fluid so as to minimize disruptions and maximize continuity. A teacher may find that using signals before a transition can help maintain students' attention and concentration and maximize the lesson's continuity. Students can also share in the responsibility for making smooth transitions by adhering to well-defined rules and playing specific roles during classroom changes. Teachers can deliberately increase student interest and curiosity before a transition, emphasize the goals and roles of the forthcoming activity, and motivate students for new and challenging experiences.

4. Use adequate and clear instructions. Presenting facts and directions clearly and information accurately, and avoiding unnecessary difficulties or misleading activities also increases active student involvement. It is hard for students to become actively involved when they're not sure what is expected of them or if they're confused or distracted. Learning opportunities that help students relate their existing knowledge to new learning tasks also maintain active participation.

Organization of instruction and instructional materials helps students focus on the essential ideas of a learning task. Learning experiences and materials can be organized in a number of ways; sequential organization, topic organization, or chronological organization are only a few of the possibilities. A clear framework for new ideas and concise directions and instruction are necessary for active involvement of students in the learning process.

5. Increase the interest value of instruction. Classroom instruction about matters of interest to students, of course, motivates them to participate actively. Therefore, teachers and curriculum developers must identify students' interests and relate them to the instruction and materials. Naturally, students are the most direct source of information about the things that interest them.

How To Improve Individual Student Involvement

1. Identify and help the least involved students. A teacher needs to observe students during instruction to identify those who have the greatest difficulty becoming actively engaged. However, simply to identify them is not enough. The teacher must determine the reasons for their lack of participation and how to evoke more active participation. Students may be uninvolved for different reasons—boredom, anxiety, fatigue, personal problems, inability to understand the instruction, or involvement in matters unrelated to the classroom. Sometimes the teacher's interest in students and their needs or "private attention" can improve motivation and involvement.

2. Prepare students adequately. School learning is cumulative and in many ways hierarchical. In order to learn a certain subject, a student must have the relevant and necessary prerequisites for each new learning task.

In the primary grades, these prerequisite knowledges and skills are derived mainly from within the subject matter being taught. In the later school grades, a wider range of prerequisite knowledge and skills may be required.

The teacher needs to find various ways of gathering evidence about students' preparedness for particular learning tasks and provide opportunities for students to obtain the prerequisites. Tests during the learning process, summaries of learned material, and reviews all give the teacher information about student progress and areas in which improvement is needed.

3. Adapt instruction to individual needs. Students vary greatly not only in their cognitive readiness for particular tasks, but also in their pace of learning, motivation to learn, anxiety, self-confidence, and self-concept as students. These factors are essential components in students' efforts and willingness to concentrate and take an active role in learning. Teachers can adapt to individual students' needs by using examples linked to students' actual and potential interests and by using a variety of practice exercises or explanations that differ in complexity.

It is possible that a highly motivated student can become apathetic and disinterested in learning due to personal problems. Or, a student who was once uninvolved could become more participating. Thus, teachers need to adapt optimal conditions of learning and instruction in a flexible way. As time passes, the same procedures that once helped a particular student may become decreasingly effective and need to be modified.

2. Feedback- Corrective Procedures

Anyone who has ever taught knows the difficulties of evaluating student learning outcomes. Students want to know whether they have passed or failed, and teachers want to know whether the goals were accomplished by the instructional processes and materials they used. Each teacher feels responsible for an appropriate, meaningful, and precise interpretation of test results; but both the teacher and the students are aware that evaluation reveals strengths and weaknesses of *instruction* as well as *learning*.

Students are not always able to evaluate their own responses. They usually benefit from information that confirms appropriate or correct responses and identifies incorrect or inappropriate ones. They vary greatly with regard to their expectations, self-esteem, anxiety, and motivation about learning and achievement.

Suppose two students in the same classroom were informed that 80 percent of their responses were correct. While one student may be disappointed with this result, another student may feel quite satisfied and gain the confidence to do even better in the future. The obvious differences between these two students are their attitudes and expectations. Some students will relearn the material they have missed and try to correct their mistakes; others may ignore their mistakes but resolve to be more attentive in the future. Still others may become discouraged, decrease their efforts, and lose interest in their work.

Each evaluation of student learning has informational as well as emotional consequences that influence students' learning and attitudes toward the learning process and themselves. In searching for the classroom conditions under which students and their teachers can make the best use of evaluative results, certain questions are raised. To what extent do teachers and students use evaluative results to alter instructional and learning outcomes? What information is needed to improve further learning and instruction? How can teachers and students use this information to optimize learning outcomes?

14

The Concept of Feedback

The term feedback is associated with electronics and computer science; it refers to a process whereby data are fed back to a system in order to modify conditions and maintain a predetermined equilibrium in the system. When we set a thermostat at a desired room temperature, it constantly receives feedback that allows it to control the temperature by switching a heater on and off.

Feedback is widely used today by most of us in a variety of daily situations. When we examine our bank account, paint a picture, or tutor a student, we judge the results according to an expected or desired standard. If we spend more money than we budgeted, if the mixture of colors does not satisfy our aesthetic values, or if the student doesn't understand our instruction, we will probably try to do something to make the situation come closer to our standard.

Belief in our ability to alter behaviors, our desire to achieve certain goals, and awareness of the means by which we can achieve predetermined standards are powerful factors in learning and development. Indeed, many educators emphasize the essential function of feedback in the learning and instructional process. Nuthall (1976) stressed the crucial importance of feedback: "If there ever arises the 'teachable moment' in class discussion or other instructional situations, it is that period following a pupil's response to a question" (p. 280).

Feedback has been used synonymously with the term "knowledge of results," which doesn't really convey the full meaning of feedback. Thorndike (1931) suggests that knowledge of results improves student performance only when the student is motivated, when the knowledge of results is informative, and when the student is helped to correct his or her mistakes. Bruner (1968) emphasizes that student learning depends on the knowledge of results "at a time when and at a place where the knowledge can be used for correction" (p. 50). This implies that knowledge of results is only one of several components included in an effective learning feedback process. In his theory of school learning, Bloom (1976) refers to this essential component of learning and instruction as feedback and corrective procedures.

Feedback and Correction in Relation to a Performance Standard

Feedback and correction involves three related components. First, it includes a definition of a standard of performance for a student, class, or teacher. Second, it involves a process whereby precise, relevant, and valid evidence are gathered and reported to the students and the teacher. This provides information regarding what has been achieved and what is still needed to be learned or taught in order to reach a defined standard. Finally, it includes the use of corrective procedures by which gaps in the learning, mistakes, and other misunderstandings can be relearned or corrected.

Setting a defined standard is essential to the feedback-corrective cycle. A predetermined standard sets the criterion to which a teacher or the students can refer in order to judge their learning and instructional results. Ideally, a predetermined standard indicates a minimum or optimal performance level to enhance students' future learning and performance. Thus, when knowledge of a student's performance is being compared with an explicit criterion, it indicates to the teacher and the student whether or not the student is ready to continue learning successfully. In contrast, when knowledge of a student's performance is given without relation to a specific and well-defined criterion, neither the teacher nor the student can determine the student's readiness for further learning.

Feedback on what has and has not been achieved is essential for modifying the learning process. The teacher can alter the instruction or materials and adapt the learning objectives or segments of instruction that have not been effective. It also orients both the teacher and the students to the strengths and weaknesses of the instruction and the learning process.

To be effective, feedback evidence must be followed by a corrective process, the stage in which students are provided with additional learning opportunities to reach to preset standard. Its main function is either to correct students' mistakes and misunderstandings or to improve their performance level on the learning objectives. Used appropriately, corrective procedures help students improve their learning and take over the corrective functions themselves.

Setting performance standards, providing students with feedback information, and following up with corrective procedures form a cycle of activities. Each of these three components plays its own role in improving learning and instruction and each requires different kinds of behaviors and activities. The strength of these three components, however, depends on their interrelatedness. Setting performance standards alone does not improve learning and instruction unless the two additional conditions and activities are involved. Providing specific and informative feedback is necessary but it has little effect on learning unless students are given opportunities to correct their difficulties and reach the preset standard.

Figure 2 demonstrates the relationships of the feedback corrective system. The performance standard typically sets the criterion required for further adequate learning, and the interplay between the feedback and corrective procedures leads to the attainment of the desired standard. The strength of this system is that it actually alters the process of learning and the process of instruction.

Figure 2. Relationships Among Components of the Feedback-Corrective System

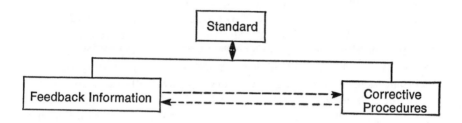

In order to be effective, the system should be used during the learning and instructional process. Feedback and corrective procedures (in relation to a preset standard) are needed at regular intervals during the learning process before errors and misunderstandings accumulate. If errors are allowed to build up, students become frustrated about their learning abilities and teachers become discouraged about their teaching abilities.

The Effects of Feedback and Corrective Procedures on Learning

Much evidence supports the powerful contribution of feedback and corrective procedures to learning effectiveness and student performance (Anderson, 1973; Arlin, 1973; Binor, 1974; Block, 1970). These procedures are at the heart of the mastery learning strategy. Two studies illustrate the effects of feedback and correction. One was carried out under laboratory conditions (Wentling, 1973), the other under regular classroom conditions (Levin, 1979).

Wentling examined how feedback and corrective procedures affect both student achievement and retention. One group of students learned eight units under conditions where no explicit standard was set prior to their learning and no feedback and corrective procedures were provided. The students were told that a test for grading purposes would follow each particular unit, for which they received only their scores.

The second group of students learned the same units, but they were required to reach a preset standard of 80 percent on each learning unit. Feedback and corrective procedures, which required the students to review their weaknesses using the same instructional materials again, helped those who failed to meet the preset standard. Following this review, students were retested with a parallel form of the unit achievement test.

At the end of the eight learning units, students in both groups took a final achievement test and a retention test. Wentling's results, when measured on the final achievement test and the retention test, indicated significant advantages in favor of the students who were provided with feedback and corrective procedures in relation to a standard.

In the Levin (1979) study, two groups of students learned a set of concepts and rules in probability. Students in one group were required to learn each unit to a predetermined performance standard (85 percent). At the end of a unit, the students were tested on their mastery of basic and important issues. On the next day, students individually received feedback information about what they had learned well and what they still needed to learn to reach the preset standard. When a mistake was made by more than half the students, the teacher reviewed the relevant concept or ideas with all the students in the class. Otherwise, the students who failed to reach the standard were assigned corrective procedures, which they completed by themselves or with other students. They received information regarding other sources of instructional materials they could use during the corrective process. These included textbooks and an alternative set of programmed learning units with detailed explanations of each concept, procedure, and rule. Students were encouraged to learn in small groups and to help each other correct their mistakes. They formed their own study groups and planned their learning procedures by themselves. Sometimes they consulted the teacher or a student who had reached the required standard. When they finished the corrective procedure, they were tested again, this time on a parallel form of the first test. Some students in this group needed to be cycled twice through the feedback corrective system until they reached the preset standard.

Students in the second group learned the same units, but without the three components of the feedback corrective system. In this group, students learned a particular unit, took a test on the unit, and went directly to the second unit in the series. When both groups finished learning the units, they were given a final summative test and tested for their ability to apply the learned rules in a variety of new situations.

This study demonstrates that students in the feedback and corrective group learned more than the students who were deprived of feedback and correction. In addition, if students learn a set of rules under learning conditions that do not include feedback and corrective procedures, their ability to apply the rules is very limited and approaches only a chance level score. In contrast, students provided with feedback and corrective procedures are able to apply the rules in new problem situations.

Block and Burns (1976) and Bloom (1976) report the results of a number of mastery learning studies, in which the use of feedback and corrective procedures are essential components. Many of the studies found that when students are provided with feedback and corrective procedures to reach a preset standard for each successive unit in a series of learning tasks, their final outcomes are very high. Approximately 80 percent of mastery students attain the same high level of achievement as the top 20 percent of control students. According to Bloom (1971), under more ideal conditions of feedback and correctives, as many as 90 percent of the students can achieve the same performance level reached by the top 20 percent of the students who are deprived of feedback and corrective opportunities.

Feedback and corrective procedures related to an appropriate standard help most students, regardless of intelligence or aptitude, to attain the desired educational goals. When groups of students are consistently provided with feedback and corrective procedures during a series of related tasks, they gradually need fewer corrective procedures to reach the preset standard. Students' achievement improves, as well as their learning habits. When students realize they are capable of mastering the standard set by the teacher, they develop greater self-confidence in their ability to learn and greater interest in the subject matter.

Grades

Almost all teachers use grades as an overall assessment of student learning and performance. The grading process is related to student achievement on specific tests and may represent the teacher's judgment of the student's ability, conduct, and motivation for learning. Teachers also use grades to judge instruction as well as student success. But grades do not indicate to teachers the specific weaknesses and strengths of their instruction, nor do they indicate the kinds of difficulties students have in the learning process.

In many educational systems, teachers assign grades using five levels of performance, such as A, B, C, D, F, or their numerical equivalents. Also, quite frequently, students' success or failure is determined by their rank order rather than by their success or failure to grasp essential ideas. Research findings (Bloom, 1964; Hicklin, 1962; Payne, 1963) demonstrate that some students are almost always rewarded each year with an A or B grade, whereas others are reminded annually that they are only D or F students. In such a grading system, some students are continually categorized as good, average, or poor. The grading system is highly consistent from one course to another; because grades do not help teachers improve the teaching and learning process, it is not surprising that grades at one level of education predict grades at later levels with great accuracy.

A grade may tell students whether they have reached an expected standard and where they are in comparison with their classmates. Students interpret this information in different ways; it may motivate some to work harder, but it may discourage others. Rarely are students given information or additional opportunities to alter their learning or their grades. Since grades do not indicate to pupils what they still need to learn, even the most highly motivated students have difficulty using grades as a basis for directing their own learning.

Adequacy of Responses

Some teachers use detailed feedback information to indicate to students the adequacy of their responses to questions, test items, or written exercises. In some classes, this approach may be served by learning materials, such as the questions at the end of a textbook chapter, programmed instruction, or by using teaching machines. Such specific information indicates to students the questions or exercises they were able to solve and those they were unable to solve. However, it is not usually related to an explicit standard, nor does it usually suggest the necessary corrective procedures.

Many studies demonstrate that knowledge of correct and incorrect results of each specific item in a learning or testing situation has *little or no effect* in improving learning (Angell, 1949; Karabinus, 1966; Karraker, 1967; Plowman and Stroud, 1942; Sassenrath and Garverick, 1965; Spencer and Barker, 1969; Sturges, 1969). According to Sturges (1972a, 1972b), information regarding the accuracy of each response is too specific and does not give students a general perspective of what they have or have not learned.

Encouragement and Criticism

Students' motivation to learn and their perceptions of teachers' expectations should have some effect on their learning. As a result, many devoted teachers feel responsible and look for different ways of developing student interest, self-confidence, and positive attitudes. While some teachers consider grades as motivating devices, others look for additional types of motivation and encouragement. These may include approval or disapproval, verbal praise or criticism, and various evaluations of student learning.

Studies over the years point to at least 180 different types of feedback behaviors at the disposal of teachers (Zahorik, 1968), who actually use only about fifteen of them. Studies tend to categorize teacher behaviors as criticism and approval; while teachers' criticism may impair learning, approval behaviors are likely to improve learning and performance.

Praise

Researchers have looked at teachers' use of praise and criticism to determine whether these variables have any effect on student learning. Contrary to expectations, there are no consistent and strong relationships between praise or criticism and student achievement. Frequent praise is not related to student achievement (Rosenshine, 1971b), nor is criticism negatively related to achievement (Flanders, 1970; Harris and others, 1968; Wright and Nuthall, 1970).

Most researchers now believe teachers' verbal behavior should be considered in light of the *information* it conveys to students (Nuthall, 1976). It must be clear to students why they are being praised or criticized and how they should modify their behavior. Many recent studies regard feedback and correctives as essential components of effective instruction (Stallings, 1976; Gage, 1976). For example, Stallings found that in classrooms where teachers systematically used a pattern of feedback and corrective processes and some praise, students attained high performance levels in reading and mathematics. The most effective pattern of teaching behavior was acknowledgement or praise for correct responses and further probing by the teachers when the answers were wrong.

Written Comments

Group instruction makes it difficult for the teacher to praise or criticize each individual student. To overcome this difficulty, many teachers provide their students with written comments on homework assignments, tests, or worksheets.

Research carried out in different subject areas and with a variety of students has studied the effects on later learning of written comments accompanied by students' grades or scores (Allen, 1972; Hake, 1973; Klinger, 1971; Mapel, 1970; Moody, 1970; Rhoads, 1967; Shrago, 1970; Simons, 1971; Starkey, 1971; Sweet, 1966). The earliest, a study by Page (1958), involved 2,139 students and 74 teachers. Each student received a grade and a teacher's comment. The comments were general and encouraging, such as "good work," "poor work but you can do better," and so forth. Page found that students who were graded on an objective test and given an encouraging comment performed better on a subsequent examination than students who received only their test grades without comments.

However, later studies failed to show a significant relationship between teacher comments and later student learning. Even when effects were established, they were small and of negligible importance (Hammer, 1972; Lesner, 1967). One study by Stewart and White (1976) explored whether written comments alone would have an effect on later student performance. They suggest that the comment in relation to a letter grade, not the comment itself, may affect student performance.

General and positive evaluative comments accompanied by a letter grade do not specify to students what they have already learned and what they still need to learn. Even if such comments could encourage students to relearn, they do not help students interpret and understand what they should do in the relearning process. Comments in conjunction with grades or scores are likely to have a more substantial effect if, instead of being general and evaluative, they provide specific feedback information.

The literature emphasizes that if students are deprived of standards, feedback, and corrections, some may learn well, but most will accumulate errors and achieve much less than they might. In addition, if only one of the three components is used, learning can improve only to a small degree and for only a few of the students. The strength of each component is complete only if all three components are involved and clearly relate to each other. Feedback, followed by opportunities for students to relearn or correct their mistakes to reach the preset standard, significantly improves most students' learning.

Setting Performance Standards

A defined performance standard sets the criterion for judging learning and instruction. Performance standards need to be set at frequent intervals during instruction. Standards that are defined in terms of student performance at the end of a semester or an academic year tell teachers and students whether the learning and instruction were effective. A performance standard used as part of the instructional process, however, indicates to the teacher the *extent* to which learning and instruction were effective and the likelihood that future instruction and learning will also be effective and efficient. Similarly, a preset standard that is explicit tells students whether they have reached the goals set by the teacher. It indicates that something needs to be done to meet the required standard if further learning is to be effective; it directs and guides students' attention and learning.

Block (1970) examined the effects of different standards on students' performance and attitudes toward the subject matter. He used five comparable groups of students and provided each with similar instruction and learning materials; each group, though, was given a different performance standard. Block found that higher standards resulted in higher cognitive outcomes. The group of students who reached the highest standard (95 percent) performed better on their knowledge of learning materials, their application of knowledge in new situations, and their retention of learning when compared with students who had reached the lower standards of 85, 75, 65, and 50 percent.

But Block also found that when the required performance standard became too high, student attitudes and interest in the subject matter decreased when compared to students who reached a somewhat lower standard. Thus, very high performance standards, when followed by feedback and corrective procedures, are effective in improving cognitive learning outcomes, but they may not have the same maximum effect on the affective outcomes of student learning. It is preferable to search for a standard that maximizes the cognitive outcomes and still maintains high affective consequences of learning.

There is no one single standard that is optimal for every learning situation and for all students. In fact, teachers are relatively free to determine not only the level of the standard, but also whether to use a single standard for all or varied standards for each student in the class. Furthermore, a teacher can decide to successively raise standards by starting somewhat lower and slowly increasing them as the course proceeds.

Most researchers do not regard 100 percent mastery of the materials as a necessary standard in the classroom. The standard should be determined by the level of achievement on one unit of learning, which is necessary to assure student success on a subsequent unit. For example, an 80 percent performance level on a learning unit may be an adequate standard if it covers the essential objectives as well as those necessary for future learning. This distinction between less relevant and more relevant objectives to subsequent learning helps teachers set realistic, practical, and effective standards.

Effective Feedback Procedures

Feedback tells students and teachers what has or has not been achieved in relation to a defined standard. The main concern should be on what has been learned and what must still be learned. A present standard indicates to students what level they are to achieve, and effective feedback information indicates whether or not they have met the standard and what they still must do to reach it. Relevant and effective feedback needs to be specific and clear in view of the learning materials and the preset standard. Feedback must also be given on a regular basis at meaningful intervals in the instructional sequence.

When feedback is used at the end of a semester or marking period, it has little value in improving student learning or teacher instruction. At this point in the learning process, errors have already accumulated and students may be less motivated to do something about the misunderstood or unlearned materials. Similarly, if the feedback information is used after a long period of time, it is not at all practical for the teacher to alter or strengthen the instruction or the instructional materials. Timing is essential to an effective use of feedback (Nuthall, 1976); it should be provided when improvement is still possible.

Within mastery learning studies, feedback information is provided to students at scheduled and defined points in a sequence of learning units. Typically, a unit of learning includes a period of about two weeks. At the end of such a period, feedback is gathered with the use of short formative tests on the major objectives of the learning units to help students determine what they still must learn. Assignments (writing an essay, planning a project, or experiments and observations) may also be potential sources of feedback evidence. In fact, every question that a student asks or answers in class could indicate that he or she has difficulties or has reached an expected standard. Pointing out mistakes is useful only if students are also helped to understand what they can do to correct them. Emphasizing what students have learned is more likely to encourage them and give them confidence in their ability to learn.

Alternative Corrective Procedures

Feedback information can be effective if, and only if, it is followed by corrective procedures which correct weaknesses of learning and instruction. In this stage, students are expected to narrow the gap between their existing performance level and the level required by the standard. Corrective procedures clear up misunderstandings students have already learned and allow them to relearn anything they have forgotten or failed to learn in the past (Bloom, 1976).

A thorough analysis of student learning and performance, coupled with analysis of the learned materials, is the key to selecting corrective procedures. One procedure allows students to review the same content materials they used previously. Although such procedures are effective in improving students' learning (Smith and Wick, 1976), they also have some limits. Sometimes inadequate or unclear learning materials cause students' mistakes; thus, reviewing the same materials may not be efficient.

Effective corrective procedures may use alternative instructional materials and methods (Block and Tierney, 1974; Block, 1972; Block and Anderson, 1975; Kersh, 1971) to help students correct their difficulties.

Using a variety of materials or methods suggests that students' weaknesses may be determined by the quality of the instruction. It also helps them understand that they may need different means to reach a performance level.

When students receive appropriate guidance, they are capable of using corrective procedures on their own. In most mastery learning studies where group instruction is used, the teacher reviews and explains items that the majority (65 percent or more) of the students missed. The remaining items are corrected by the students individually or in small study groups.

The most effective corrective procedure for students above the second grade involves small study groups of two or three. Students find the questions they missed, and the students who answered them correctly take turns explaining the correct answers (Bloom, 1978). If all the students in a small study group answered a question incorrectly, they can refer to supplementary materials or seek help from the teacher or a student from another group.

If the groups are heterogeneous in terms of student achievement and motivation, the corrective process may become cooperative when no single student acts as the "tutor" for the others. Underlying the strength of such a corrective process are similar experiences and language shared by the students.

The corrective process is the stage in which students have additional opportunities to reach the preset standard and should be followed by further feedback information. In mastery learning classes, under group instruction, corrective procedures are followed by additional formative testing. Typically, a teacher uses a new parallel test covering objectives or items students had to relearn or correct. Students receive evidence about whether they have reached the set standard, what they have learned successfully, and what they still need to learn. As a result, students begin to develop a positive view of their own learning abilities (Bloom, 1976, 1977).

Students who have more self-confidence and a greater desire to learn become more involved as they progress in their learning. Gradually, they need less external help to reach a defined standard and may even take over the corrective procedures themselves. Effective use of feedback corrective systems helps teachers develop more confident students who not only achieve at a higher level but who also *learn how to learn.*

3. Instructional Cues

The essence of classroom instruction creates situations that stimulate successful learning. Each educational situation is full of possibilities for both the teacher and the students. Each includes a variety of stimuli that convey to students the content elements to be learned and directions for what they are to do and how they are to do it. These explanations and directions are referred to as *instructional cues* (Bloom, 1976).

The major cues in group instruction tend to be verbal, directing students in certain activities or particular ideas. Other cues use students' perceptual, visual, tactile, or other senses in the learning process. Colors or maps, diagrams, models, or film are some of the nonverbal instructional cues teachers and curriculum developers use.

In analyzing our own teaching, we may recognize that we use a particular pattern of explanation whenever we introduce a new topic. Or we may use certain words or tones to emphasize an important issue or to contrast it with previously learned issues. Different instructional cues are used for different educational goals. Teachers use particular instructional cues, such as repetition or drill exercises, whenever students are to remember certain ideas, concepts, or procedures. Teachers use instructional cues such as probing or juxtaposition of ideas or procedures when they want students to understand and use ideas in novel situations.

Much research has focused on the direct relationship between instructional cues and learning outcomes (Dunkin and Biddle, 1974; Gage, 1976; Rosenshine, 1971a, 1971b). Recently, educators and researchers have recognized that, for a better understanding of the role and effects of instructional cues, cues should be considered in terms of the activities or behaviors they elicit in students during the learning process (Doyle, 1978).

Instructional cues are effective in improving learning if they satisfy two related sets of conditions. They must be clear to students and they must elicit intended reactions or responses. If a teacher speaks too rapidly or uses strange words, the students will have difficulty responding to the cues. Under these conditions, we would not expect the desired learning to occur. If a teacher uses familiar words at an appropriate pace, students will be able to respond. If directions or explanations are relevant and help students learn, students' response to such cues should result in improved learning.

Instructional cues focus student attention on the important and critical issues and offer opportunities to actually experience behaviors that can improve learning.

Educational Objectives

Educational objectives describe and illustrate the behaviors and processes that students are expected to acquire. According to Tyler (1949), the most useful and clear way of stating objectives is to indicate the content to be taught and learned and the kind of behaviors to be developed. For example, the ability to remember capital cities is a specific educational objective that includes two dimensions: content (names of cities) and behavior (remembering).

Educational objectives can improve the teaching process. Objectives guide teachers in thinking about and planning learning experiences and help them in selecting and developing methods and materials that are likely to produce the intended learning.

A substantial number of studies have investigated the effect of student knowledge of learning objectives on achievement. Most of these studies were made under learning conditions that approximate classroom situations (Blaney and McKie, 1969; Davis, 1970; Duchastel and Brown, 1974; Engel, 1968; Gagné and Rothkopf, 1975; Rothkopf and Kaplan, 1972; Royer, 1977). They generally indicate that students who are given information about instructional objectives prior to their learning remember the learning materials better than students who are told nothing about objectives. Also, *specific* objectives have the greatest effect on learning (Kaplan, 1976; Kaplan and Rothkopf, 1974; Kaplan and Simmons, 1974).

Some researchers, however, question the value of objectives as effective cues for learning (Brown, 1970; DeRose, 1970; Ebel, 1967; Eisner, 1967; Etter, 1969; Jackson and Beford, 1965; Smith, 1967). It is clear that providing objectives to students is advantageous under some conditions, but not all conditions. Simply providing students with objectives is not enough.

Melton (1978) emphasizes that when objectives are too general or ambiguous, extremely difficult, or ignored by students, just knowing the objectives will have little or no effect on student learning. Also, if students are not interested in the objectives or if they are already motivated to learn, advance knowledge of instructional objectives will do nothing to enhance their learning. Effective instructional objectives need to be clear, not too difficult, and stated prior to instruction.

Gagné and Rothkopf (1975) and Rothkopf and Koether (1978) explored the relationship between objectives and the characteristics of learning materials. Objectives are more effective when they emphasize the same things emphasized in the instructional materials.

Objectives that are given to students prior to instruction function as orienting stimuli (Duchastel and Brown, 1974). They focus students' attention on the relevant materials and processes and help determine students' study habits, organization, and processing procedures (Gagné and others, 1977). For instance, Gagné observed a group of students who were provided with a statement of educational goals and instructional material. Several of these students first read the goals and the instructional material; then reread the goals and material again to find forgotten information; and finally looked at the goals, closed their eyes, and mouthed words as if using the goals to cue their review. Thus, the goals helped the students organize their learning materials and concentrate on the relevant information.

An intriguing and somewhat different approach was suggested by LaPorte and Nath (1976). They found that comparable groups of students who were asked to master a different number of objectives showed differences in achievement. Those who were asked to achieve more objectives actually did so, as opposed to the students who were asked to achieve fewer learning objectives. According to LaPorte and Nath, after receiving instructional goals, a student develops a standard of performance and acquires information until she or he has attained the standard. When students were instructed to do their best, they set a low performance goal, far below their maximum capabilities. But when students were required to master the maximum number of goals, their incentives as well as their learning increased. This indicates that when students are told specifically what is expected of them, they are likely to make the expectations their standards for learning.

Instructional goals typically emphasize the most important aspects for both immediate and future learning. Students' knowledge of the goals gives them a sure sense of what they are to do and how they are to do it, and enables them to judge when they have accomplished their task. Clear statements of educational goals, which are appropriately related to instruction, are powerful instructional cues for teachers and students. Using instructional goals effectively does facilitate student learning.

Questions

Teachers use questions as a teaching method to receive feedback about whether students understand what is being taught, whether the instruction is effective, and when it should be changed. Researchers have estimated that between 300 and 400 questions are asked in a typical school day (Gall, 1970; Floyd, 1960; Schreiber, 1967; Stevens, 1912). Because of individualized instructional strategies in the elementary grades, there is less time for teachers' questions and more emphasis on questions written in learning materials. However, in higher grades and in different levels of science programs, classroom questions are still a very important aspect of learning and instruction (Rice, 1977).

Questions can be classified according to the cognitive processes that are required to answer them. Memory and recall of specific facts or knowledge are stimulated by about 60 percent of the teacher's questions. Only about 20 percent of the questions stimulate students' independent and critical thinking (Arnold and others, 1973; Corey, 1940; Floyd, 1960; Gallagher, 1965; Haynes, 1935; Wilson, 1969; Tinsley and others, 1970).

The frequency of factual questions in the classroom is positively related to students' performance on test items that measure factual knowledge (Rosenshine, 1979). Surprisingly, though, higher mental process questions do not relate consistently to student achievement. For instance, some studies (Hunkins, 1967; Furst, 1967; Soar, 1966) claim that such a relationship does exist to a significant extent, while others demonstrate that classroom questions requiring divergent thinking (Wright and Nuthall, 1970) or other kinds of higher mental process questions (Spaulding, 1965) are unrelated to student performance.

Based on a thorough review of the literature, Rosenshine (1976) concludes that the results of these studies could best be stated as trends suggesting that lower order questions tend to be positively related to achievement, while high order classroom questions tend to be unrelated to achievement. These findings and conclusions contradict educators' and researchers' assumptions that the types of questions used in classrooms directly determine students' level of thinking. We need to recognize, however, that most of these studies did not relate students' responses to the teacher's questions, nor did they determine whether the questions are likely to be effective instructional cues only if they are clear or whether they stimulate appropriate student answers and behaviors.

We could reasonably assume, on the other hand, that if a teacher asks a higher mental process question to which students do not appropriately respond, such questions will have little effect on the intended learning.

Similarly, if students do respond appropriately to higher levels of questions, the questions will directly affect learning and performance.

There are studies to support these assumptions. First, a number of research studies demonstrate that there is a positive relationship between the level of thinking required by teachers' questions and the cognitive process actually manifested in students' responses (Arnold and others, 1973; Gallagher, 1965; Marshall and Mood, 1972; Miller, 1966; Taba and others, 1964). Second, more recent research indicates that students' responses to academic questions are positively related to student achievement (Stallings and Kaskowitz, 1974). Brophy and Evertson (1976) found a strong positive relationship between the correctness of students' responses to teachers' questions and student achievement. Clearly, more research is needed to establish the relationship between the nature of teachers' questions, the correctness of student responses, and student learning outcomes.

It does seem that the types of questions asked can stimulate appropriate cognitive thinking processes in students. If oral questions are to be effective instructional cues, teachers and reseachers must emphasize appropriate use of questions that are clearly related to the instructional material and to the desired educational outcomes.

Much of school learning and instruction makes use of written materials. Since questions are considered central to any learning, it is not surprising to find that researchers have focused on the study of the effects of questions inserted in instructional materials. Do they stimulate appropriate answers or behaviors? Do they aid in facilitating student learning? In other words, are they effective instructional cues?

The use of questions as effective cues in a written text has been the topic of a number of experimental research studies (Rothkopf, 1972; Frase, 1970; Rothkopf and Kaplan, 1972; Frase and Schwartz, 1975). Rothkopf (1972) found that when two questions were inserted on every third page of a 36-page prose passage, retention of the passage was considerably more effective than when no such questions were used. Some of the questions were directly relevant to the questions on the retention test. Others were not. In this study, Rothkopf found that questions that were relevant to the test did facilitate performance on the test. In addition, questions that had no direct relationship to the items in the test had a general positive effect on the test performance.

Some of the studies dealt with the place in the text at which questions were inserted. In general, consistent facilitative learning effects were found when the questions were inserted after, rather than before, a prose passage (Frase, 1968; Rothkopf, 1966; Rothkopf and Bisbicos, 1967). In particular, the studies reveal better and longer recall and retention of the learned materials when the questions follow, rather than pre-ceed, the passage (Anderson and Biddle, 1975; Frase, 1970; Rothkopf, 1972; Rothkopf and Bisbicos, 1967). Questions inserted at the *end* of a passage increased recall of material not included in the questions. In con-trast, questions preceding the passage improved students' achievement primarily on the materials emphasized by the questions and had some negative effects on the learning of materials not emphasized by the ques-tions (Anderson, and Biddle, 1975; Rothkopf and Bisbicos, 1967; Frase, 1975; Rothkopf, 1966).

Several studies have explored the effects of different types of ques-tions used in instructional materials (Rickards and DiVesta, 1974; Roth-kopf and Bisbicos, 1967; Watts and Anderson, 1971; Allen, 1970; Hunkins, 1968; Tenenberg, 1969; Howe and Colley, 1976; Mayer, 1975; McConkie and others, 1973; McGraw and Grotelueschen, 1972). For example, Watts and Anderson (1971) found that questions asking students to apply principles to new problems resulted in greater learning than questions that were limited to remembering examples included in the ma-terial text. Thus, questions on higher mental processes have a greater facilitative effect on learning than do questions that require lower mental processes. Similarly, Mayer (1975) found that students required to answer complex questions excelled more on test questions relating to a new passage than did students who were asked to answer simpler questions. The results make it clear that different kinds of questions inserted in learn-ing materials can be effective instructional cues. What is the nature of the behaviors they activate in students? How do they operate as effective instructional cues?

Research literature suggests that questions inserted in instructional materials enhance learning outcomes due to a selective attention and active learning process. The questions help students learn more effectively and efficiently by reducing irrelevant activity during learning and increasing students' awareness of the expected goals of instruction. Questions moti-vate students to rehearse and selectively review the relevant material (Frase, 1968; Koran and Koran, 1975).

The use of questions in instructional materials does not simply pro-vide students with answering skills (Mayer, 1975). The questions indi-cate to students what they are to do and how they are to do it, giving them greater control over their own learning processes. When the ques-tions are at an appropriate level of difficulty for the students, they are very effective instructional cues for improving learning (Hiller, 1974).

The quality of questions and their location in the text determine the kinds of outcomes we can expect students to achieve. This implies that the questions used in written texts should be clearly related to the goals of instruction.

Visual Aids

Most school learning is still based on written materials and largely dependent on students' reading ability. But schools have dramatically increased the use of media instructional aids such as movie equipment, kits of manipulative materials, film strips, records, diagrams, and maps. These tools enhance learning by making use of a variety of sensory processes (Carroll, 1968). Many researchers have focused on the effects of cues that make use of different sensory stimuli in the learning process.

"It is proverbial that a picture is worth 1,000 words, and there is some truth in this; on the other hand, there are instances when pictures can interfere with proper comprehension if they lead the subject to make incorrect perceptions of a situation" (Carroll, 1968, p. 8). If this is so, when would visual illustrations and demonstrations be effective instructional cues? What are the activities they elicit in students when they are effective?

May (1965), on the basis of a literature review, indicates that simplicity of pictorial presentation facilitates learning. Pictures need to draw the attention of students precisely to those aspects of learning required by the instructional goal. In fact, most of the research in this area (Travers, 1973) emphasizes clarity and simplicity of demonstrations and illustrations as necessary conditions for visual aids to be effective instructional cues. Furthermore, it is important to provide accompanying verbal descriptions and directions. Young students, in particular, try to remember as many details as possible in an illustration, many of which are not relevant to the learning goals (Ross, 1966). Older students also may use pictorial presentations ineffectively (Wesley, 1962). Descriptions prior to a demonstration aid in focusing students' attention on critical features and direct students to spend more effective time on relevant information. Verbal descriptions also help students organize the major features of the demonstration (Bandura and others, 1966).

Pictorial illustrations and demonstrations, apart from serving as attention capturing devices (Paradowski, 1967), need to be informative (Goldberg, 1974). Consequently, detailed illustrations that parallel the relevant textual information help enhance student learning. According to Goldberg, illustrations are most effective when they accompany other learning materials that are being presented for the first time or that need review. The illustrations contribute little to materials with which the students are already familiar.

Research evidence demonstrates that students' recall of information from learning materials is greatly improved if appropriate visual aids accompany verbal material (Paivio, 1969; Rohwer and Harris, 1975; Rohwer and Matz, 1975). Similarly, instructions to students to form mental pictures relating to the content being taught were found to yield significant improvement in students' recall of ideas and materials (Levin, 1973; Levin and others, 1974; Kulhavy and Swenson, 1975; Paivio, 1971; Rohwer and Ammons, 1971). The studies generally show that grade school students remember more from a text if they try to form mental images while reading the text. Visual imagery tends to be less effective in improving learning with very young students who apparently have more difficulty understanding these cues (Shimron, 1974). Similar results of visual imagery were demonstrated in the learning of principles from graphs (Lee, 1971; Lee and Dobson, 1977).

Underlining segments in a text is generally positive in facilitating student learning. Cashen and Leicht (1970), for example, found that underlining resulted in greater retention of both the underlined content and the content which was not underlined. In a study by Rickards and August (1975), students who were instructed to underline the important issues in a written text had greater retention of all the material than did the students who were provided with materials already underlined.

Several recent studies reveal that a variety of instructional materials, particularly visual and manipulative materials, can contribute to student learning (Stallings, 1976; McDonald, 1976; Greabell, 1978). Demonstrations, illustrations, and other forms of visual emphasis are effective instructional cues when they satisfy two requirements: they must be informative, clear, and simple, and they must activate desired behaviors by students.

Practice

In many schools, exercises and practice experiences make up a large part of a student's work and are communication devices used by teachers or teaching materials that require students to recall and apply their knowledge. Practice experiences refer, then, to any attempt by students to perform a learning task. It is generally agreed that practice experiences and exercises are effective in improving learning. But what kind of practices are most useful in facilitating student learning? Should the practice be uniform and similar to the learning experiences used in the classroom? Or should practice experiences be varied and differ from the experiences students have in the classrooms?

A great number of studies explored these questions. Some were performed under laboratory conditions (Duncan, 1958; Harlow, 1949, 1959) while others were conducted under classroom conditions (Gagné and Basoler, 1963; Gagné and others, 1965; Levin, 1979; Traub, 1966). Most of these studies seem to indicate that learning is more effective if students can practice in a variety of situations. When students are required to cope with frequent changes in the practice exercises, they learn to identify the essential elements in each learning task. They also learn how to adapt to changing circumstances and how to identify common patterns in learning situations. These behaviors are believed to be evoked by varied practices and to facilitate student learning and performance.

For example, Traub (1966) varied the problem context and constructed his practice exercises so that the numbers, the portion of the number lines employed, and the size of the number used was different from problem to problem. Interestingly, the group of students who practiced with heterogeneous problems made fewer stereotyped errors than did students who practiced with the homogeneous set of problems. The effectiveness of heterogeneous practice questions in this study may be due to the fact that they formed more complex learning conditions that stimulated students to learn more. The homogeneous problems, which were simpler, stimulated students to develop routine procedures of solving the problems, which resulted in more stereotyped errors.

In a study by Levin (1979), two groups of students learned a set of rules to a comparably high level. Following mastering the rules, each group received a different set of practice experiences. One type of experience included problems that were similar to those used during the learning of the rules. The questions were very limited in terms of their context, wording, and form of presentation. The second type of practice experience involved more varied problems in terms of their complexity, context, wording, and form or presentation. The results of this study demonstrated that practice with the heterogeneous set developed the students' ability to apply the learned rules to a broad range of new situations. Practice on the narrow set of homogeneous problems developed the students' ability to apply their knowledge only in a narrow range of problem situations.

It is important to recognize that although varied practice experiences are likely to be more effective than constant practice, such variability seems to be most effective under certain conditions. These conditions are to alter one element of the problems at a time (Schmidt, 1975), practice the varied dimensions in relation to a general framework, and help the students become aware of the alterations in the specific dimensions.

Under some circumstances practice on homogeneous problems also may be helpful and effective. If teachers want students to remember a skill, procedure, or principle, practice on a limited range of exercises may be useful. As long as it is not overdone (Luchins and Luchins, 1950), homogeneous practice evokes particular sets of behaviors that help students recall learned information.

Practice experiences can be effective cues for instructing students about what to do and how to do it. When these practices are clear to students, they seem to produce desired behaviors that facilitate student learning and performance in the expected direction. Varied as well as limited practice experiences can be effective instructional cues, but they constitute effective cues for different kinds of instructional goals.

How To Improve Instructional Cues

Our analysis of the research literature on instructional cues includes only a small number of activities and processes used frequently by teachers and curriculum developers. We selected those for which there is research evidence demonstrating their effects on student learning. Each kind of instructional cue discussed above has focused on a specific set of cues that can improve student learning to a significant degree. Each of these types of cues (statement of educational objectives, questions, visual aids, practice) has its own function and specific purpose at various stages in the learning process and for different kinds of educational goals.

1. Increase the variety of cues. Instructional cues differ in their strength and relevance for different students. For example, it is likely that students who are verbally competent will learn more easily with verbal cues (Cronbach and Snow, 1976). Students who feel more comfortable with graphic presentations or other forms of visual stimuli may learn more easily with such cues. Cues that are likely to evoke appropriate and relevant activities for some students may not be as effective for other students. Teachers need to be able to improve their use of cues to ensure effective learning by most students—by giving cues that involve perceptual, visual, tactile, and other senses.

2. Adapt cues to individual needs. An individualized learning situation provides an opportunity for a great deal of communication and interaction between the student and the teacher. A good teacher naturally uses a variety of cues and modifies them to the needs of the student (S. Bloom, 1976). Whenever the teacher recognizes that the student has difficulties in understanding an explanation, he or she offers a different one. The tutor is constantly shifting directions, examples, questions, or explanations. Depending on the student's behaviors and activities, the teacher clarifies or repeats examples and explanations as necessary to make them clear and to evoke the appropriate activity from the student.

The powerful effects of cues in a one-to-one learning instructional situation are brought about when the teacher not only alters the cues, but alters them in such a way that they fit the special needs of the individual student. This constant adaptation of cues to the student's needs is likely to be done so quickly and naturally that the teacher appears to be doing it unconsciously. It becomes almost like a conversation between two interested people.

3. Adapt cues to class needs. Many teachers plan their instruction and direct their attention to only a small number of students in the classroom (Dahloff, 1971; Good and Brophy, 1971). This selective group of students serves as a mirror to teachers whereby they determine the quality of cues. This evidence guides teachers in correcting cues, altering them, or providing additional cues. However, if teachers judge instructional cues by the reactions of only a few of the best students in class, the cues may not suit the needs of other students.

However, if teachers direct their attention to a small (four or five) but representative sample of students in a class, they can determine whether the cues are effective or ineffective to the entire range of students. Such a small sample can represent the entire spectrum of capabilities, interests, and attitudes of students in the class. When teachers alter the cues or provide additional ones, they are more likely to be responding to the needs of most of the students. It is desirable to change the sample of students frequently.

4. Use cues spontaneously. Using cues effectively is one of the most challenging activities for every teacher. It is also one of the most enjoyable parts of instruction. It enables teachers to use their knowledge, imagination, and experiences to help students learn. Skilled teachers develop great facility in adapting cues to a variety of circumstances and to the needs of different students.

We are familiar with an interactive situation in which a tutor almost unconsciously adapts his or her explanations, demonstrations, examples, and even the tone of voice to fit the needs of the student. This is not a highly trained skill for the tutor. Almost anyone can explain something to someone who knows less about it. A preplanned scenario of words or activities is not very useful. The interactive process is the key to the effectiveness of any one-to-one relation in learning or in any communication process in which two persons participate.

An instructional situation which involves a single student may be little different than a two-way conversation. But when teaching involves a class of 20 to 30 students, a more complex interactive process takes place. Effective use of cues in the class cannot be specifically planned in advance. Its effectiveness stems from the constant efforts of the students and the teacher to communicate about what is to be learned and how it is to be done. It is a natural and spontaneous process in which a teacher converses with all the students, while being sensitive to the different needs signaled by the members of the class.

When cues are clear and adapted to different students, they evoke the appropriate learning activities in the students. Under these conditions cues can be instrumental in improving learning of all the students. The joy of teaching and learning is in this spontaneous interaction.

4. Evaluating Instruction

After new instructional processes have been introduced, their effectiveness and quality must be maintained. Over time, use of the processes improves. Teachers gain experience and adjust to new management and instructional procedures. Students become more familiar with new content and methods. Teachers, administrators, and supervisors all assume responsibility for implementing the processes and are able to identify difficulties. This information usually serves as a basis for teachers to correct or improve their effectiveness; it enables them to assess how well the corrective actions worked and to gain insight into the process of instruction and learning. In fact, they accept the responsibility for evaluation and assume the role of evaluators.

In our daily lives we evaluate our environment, instruction, behavior, or change in behavior. Yet, a distinction should be made between informal and formal evaluation. We informally evaluate a lesson we taught or watched when we say "this was a good lesson." We informally evaluate our own behavior when we say that we are not proficient enough at organizing classroom discussion. We informally evaluate an instructional experience when we say that participation in a simulation game helped us become more proficient in listening to students. These are statements of our decisions and judgments. They do not involve an explicit description of our experiences, nor do they entail the basic data or values that led us to these decisions or judgments. In *informal* evaluation, it is enough that the judgment is made explicit (Wittrock, 1970).

Intelligent, informal evaluation is based on experiences, values, and knowledge, but many educators are not satisfied with exclusive use of informal evaluation. Due to the importance and consequences of evaluation, educators look for more scientific, systematic, objective, or formal measures. Formal evaluation provides explicit statements of judgments and decisions and includes objective measures on which to base those judgments and decisions. Formal evaluation describes why and how we reach certain conclusions. For example, a teacher or a supervisor who judges a lesson favorably provides evidence he or she has collected from the students, such as their level of interest in the lesson, their judgment of its clarity, their degree of involvement, or their performance following the lesson. A teacher may very well describe the pattern of the lesson, the activities that took place, their sequence, content, level of difficulty, and so on. In this case, the teacher or the supervisor explicitly states the bases for his or her judgment.

The word "evaluation" is commonly used for a range of activities connected with educational practices and programs. In its broadest sense, it refers to the worth of an educational program or model, or a whole system of education. It has a more modest meaning when applied to the appraisal of a segment of instruction. While in the past, evaluation has been conceived mainly as a process of passing judgment, nowadays it is seen as a continuous process of collecting information and supplying feedback for improvement. Therefore, the role of evaluation is similar to the role of feedback-corrective procedures discussed in Chapter Two. Feedback is provided to or collected by the teacher in relation to a qualitative standard of desired classroom processes. The corrective procedures are expected to be developed and used by the teachers themselves.

Classroom Observation

The most prevalent technique for collecting information about classroom processes is classroom observation. Observational techniques have been extensively treated in educational literature. The anthology *Mirrors for Behavior* (Simon and Boyer, 1967) contains 92 observational systems. Although observation is a relatively expensive way of gathering data, compared with other techniques such as questionnaires or tests, there are certain situations in which observation is particularly useful and sometimes indispensable.

Observation normally aims at making an objective record of events or behaviors as they occur. According to Yoloye (1977), in effective observation, we need to pay attention to the relevant events or behavior, to make an objective record of the behavior, to present this record in a manner that will yield meaningful interpretation, and to interpret the data.

Observation techniques are comprised of divergent forms of data collection such as systematic-observation instruments, rating scales, unstructured observation, and audio or videotaping.

Systematic observations include all techniques in which predetermined behaviors or events are observed and recovered systematically according to predetermined schedules. Systematic observation schemes are divided into two groups: sign systems and category systems.

Sign systems describe the instructional situation as a snapshot describes a view. In a sign system attention is focused on a certain set of behaviors or phenomena; for instance, the teacher uses audio visual aids, the teacher states the objective of the lesson, the student corrects a mistake, and so forth. Typically, the instrument consists of a relatively large number of well defined behaviors. After a period of observation, all the behaviors that have occurred are checked. Behaviors that occur more than once during an observation period are checked only once. It may also be that during a whole period of observation, no signs will be made for particular behaviors.

Category systems generally deal with a more restricted number of behaviors (categories). They are usually recorded continuously, as often as they occur, in order to produce a moving record of behaviors. The observer's task is to record behavior as it occurs, perhaps every three seconds or more often. For example, to measure active learning time, a trained observer watches each student in a classroom or a representative group of students for a certain period of time. He or she then codes the observed behavior as being on-task or off-task. Sometimes these categories are broken down into a number of particular on or off-task activities such as writes, listens, asks a question, works with other students, disturbs other students, waits for the teacher, and so on. The measure of time or involvement is usually expressed as the percent of total time the student was on-task or actively involved in particular on-task behaviors. It is calculated by dividing the number of codings of behavior indicating student on-task behaviors by the total number of codings and multiplying by 100:

$$\frac{\text{number of on-task behaviors}}{\text{total number of behaviors}} \times 100$$

While such measures could be derived for each student, one can easily calculate the mean degree of involvement of active learning time for the whole classroom by averaging the measures of all students. This also estimates the degree of variability of student involvement in the class (Anderson, 1976; Lahaderne, 1968; Levin and others, 1980; Shimron, 1976).

A second procedure used to measure active learning time is the stimulated-recall procedure developed by Bloom (1953). It estimates the degree of covert involvement and generally has been used in lecture and discussion situations. Typically, a tape is made of the lecture as it is being presented to the students. As soon as possible after the lesson is completed, the tape is replayed for the students. The tape is stopped at various points of time and students are asked to recall in several sentences what they had been thinking at that moment during the lecture. Their thoughts are classified as being on-task or off-task or as being relevant or irrelevant to the lesson. In classrooms where "seatwork" is the dominant instructional setting, this procedure is modified since verbal stimulus is not constantly present in the classroom. The students are asked to stop working at various stages during the lesson and write in a sentence or two what they were thinking just prior to being told to stop. Once again, the thoughts are classified as being on-task or off-task. A measure based on the ratio of relevant thoughts (on-task) to total thoughts (relevant and nonrelevant) can then be derived (Krauskopf, 1963; Özcelik, 1973).

In large scale studies, correlational or experimental observation of active learning time or the degree of student involvement is only one observed behavior among other classroom processes. For example, in the Beginning Teacher Evaluation Study (BTES) (Marliave and others, 1977), students were observed as being engaged (asking questions, making verbal statements or responses, making written statements or responses, listening, or reading) or not engaged (socializing, misbehaving, daydreaming, waiting for help). In Solomon's study (Solomon and Kendall, 1976) of 101 observed behaviors of teachers, students, and class organization, six behaviors were directly indicative of student or class degree of involvement, including "half of class or more working intently with teacher attention," "half of class or more working intently without teacher attention," "student listening or watching," and "two or more students not paying attention to teacher when expected to."

Classroom observations are also the most prevalent technique for measuring feedback and corrective procedures as well as instructional cues. However, in contrast to procedures for observing active learning time, the target of these observations is typically the teacher or the interaction between the teacher and student. Usually, an observation scheme includes a description of teacher behaviors manifesting different kinds of feedback and corrective procedures or instructional cues. The observer is asked to watch the teacher, the class, or an interaction between teacher and students for a period of time and then to code the behaviors that occurred. For example, Zahorik (1968) classified feedback behaviors of teachers into 14 categories. Stallings (1978) includes in her observational schedule categories such as "adult acknowledges student behavior," "adult gives negative corrective feedback for task," and "adult gives negative corrective feedback for behavior." The BTES observational scheme includes such teacher feedback behaviors as: "the teacher gives information to the student about how he or she is performing where no direction or explanation is involved" (academic feedback), "the teacher asks a question or requests information from the student in order to assess academic performance" (academic monitory question), and "the teacher gives the student feedback about general, task-related behaviors but not about correctness of responses" (task engagement feedback). Anderson and others (1979) include in their observational system a number of classroom processes and teacher behaviors that measure feedback-corrective activities. These include the use of sustaining feedback, a type of feedback behavior that gives the student a second chance to correct himself; the use of terminal feedback in which the teacher supplies the correct answer or asks another student to answer; the use of process feedback in which the teacher explains to the students how to figure out an answer. Observed feedback behaviors used in this study for correct student responses include acknowledgement of student response and repetition of the correct answers.

Similarly, in order to observe instructional cues in the classroom, a list of teacher behaviors or categories of behaviors is provided to a trained observer who codes their occurrence. For example, in Solomon's study the list of teacher's activities includes several behaviors manifesting instructional cues such as "the teacher gives directions," "the teacher discusses or demonstrates use of equipment or material," "the teacher asks convergent questions," and "the teacher asks a divergent question." Anderson and others (1979) include in their observation system instructional cues such as the use of overview or introductory activities for the lesson, the use of demonstrations, and types of questions.

The most common measure used in most studies is the *frequency* (usually in percentages) of feedback-corrective procedures and instructional cues. A measure that is particularly useful when the category system of observation is used is *timing* of the recorded behavior during the lesson. Other measures are an index of the *variety* of the behaviors used, and the degree or level of *adaptability* of the behaviors to different students in the classroom.

Rating Scales

Rating scales are subjective assessments made on an established scale. They are particularly useful for behaviors that cannot be easily recorded in discrete terms and therefore cannot be easily quantified by counting procedures. For example, an observer may be asked to provide information on the degree to which the teacher pays attention to the needs of individual students or the extent to which a student cooperates with classmates. For such purposes, the observer needs to observe over a period of time several behaviors or events that may occur simultaneously and later quantify these attributes in terms of ratings.

Figure 3. Rating Scales for Measuring Instructional Cues

Complexity of Communication Scale:

1	2	3	4	5	6	7

Teacher-student interaction concentrates on factual information. Questions require mostly recall.

Teacher-student interaction contains some higher-order questions. "Hows" and "whys" sometimes required.

Teacher-student interaction involves high proportion of higher-order questions. Students required to apply, interpret, evaluate, and synthesize.

Structuring Scale:

1	2	3	4	5	6	7

Instruction characterized by *absence* of outlining of content, stating objectives, signaling transitions, indicating important points, reviewing, and summarizing.

Instruction sometimes characterized by structuring behavior. Some aspects of structuring may be present and others may not be present.

Instruction characterized by outlining of content, stating objectives, signaling transitions, indicating important points, reviewing, and summarizing.

Clarity Scale:

1	2	3	4	5	6	7

Teacher is not understood by students. Teacher language is overly complex or ambiguous. Students' questions do not get answered adequately.

Teacher is understood by students about half the time.

Teacher's communication understood by students. Students' questions are answered clearly.

Flexibility Scale:

1	2	3	4	5	6	7

Lessons are implemented without changes.

Daily activities are moderately flexible.

Teacher changes activities to suit students' mood changes and other conditions.

The more common method involves rating various attributes or behaviors by checking such terms as "outstanding," "above average," "average," "below average," and "unsatisfactory." Other methods for structuring the scale include numbers increasing from one up to five or more, when one is the lowest rating indicating very poor and five is the highest indicating very good. Ordinarily, a rating form will include certain statements that specify the behaviors corresponding to the various points on the rating form.

For example, in measuring active learning time or the degree of student involvement, an observer may rate the extent or the quality of student participation on a scale of one to five points, where one refers to the student having never been on-task and five refers to the student having been consistently on-task. This measure of involvement is not in terms of amount or percent of time at all. It is, rather, a more subjective report which measures how well the student has spent his or her time.

Similarly, in measuring instructional cues or feedback-corrective procedures, it is possible to construct an appropriate and relevant rating scale and to ask an observer to use it at the end of an observed lesson or at particular times during the lesson. The BTES uses several 7-point rating scales, some of which actually measure instructional cues. One scale item, Complexity of Community, measures the complexity of the verbal interaction between the teacher and students. If the interactions require mental processes beyond recall of knowledge, then the communication is relatively complex. The seven end of the scale is represented by communication that involves many high mental process questions. Figure 3 shows examples of four BTES scales.

Rating scales measure the quality of cues used in one lesson or an average of cues used in several lessons. They do not measure frequency, variety, or adaptability of feedback-corrective procedures for individual students. If these measures are important to the teacher or evaluator, specific scales should be developed.

Student Questionnaires

Another prevalent technique for collecting information about classroom processes is the use of student questionnaires. The questions may be open-ended, requiring respondents to answer in their own words, or multiple-choice, requiring repondents to select one or more answers from among those provided. It is also possible to provide the respondents with checklists or rating scales.

Questionnaires have several advantages: they are relatively inexpensive to administer; they can be administered at a convenient or relevant time during the class; they can be designed to maintain respondents' anonymity; and they can be standardized. Student questionnaires are particularly useful for teachers since they do not require an outside observer. Underlying the approach of student self-report questionnaires is the belief that students themselves form a group of sensitive, well informed judges of their classroom process. Their reports may, then, serve as a mirror for the teacher.

In a study by Gage (1976) on teacher effectiveness in explaining, students rated the lesson on the following aspects of instructional processes derived from the Stanford Teacher Competence Appraisal Guide: clarity of aims, organization of the lecture, beginning the lecture, clarity of presentation, pacing the lecture, pupil attention, ending the lecture, teacher-pupil rapport, and amount of learning. For each dimension, the ratings were made on a 7-point scale ranging from "truly exceptional" to "weak" with an additional category for "unable to observe."

After each lesson, students described their degree of involvement in an Attention Report:

During this lecture, my mind wandered and I began to think about other things:
- (0) all of the time
- (1) most of the time
- (2) some of the time
- (3) a little bit of the time
- (4) none of the time

Similarly, Brown and Holtzman (1967) asked students to respond "true" or "false" to items on the Survey of Study Habits and Attitudes, which deal with student activities during and after group instruction. It includes such items as:

(a) I do not bother to correct errors on the papers my teacher grades and returns.
(b) I find myself taking down unimportant notes during class.
(c) I hesitate to ask the teacher for further explanation of an assignment that is not clear to me.

A similar approach has been used by Hecht (1977), who developed an activities checklist consisting of 53 short statements. For each statement, the student has to indicate if the statement applied to his or her thoughts and actions during class or if it did not apply. The student must respond to every item. The statements are concerned with four aspects of classroom processes: the effectiveness of instructional cues, feedback-corrective procedures, student participation (involvement), and reinforcement.

Content Analysis

Much of school learning and instruction involves written materials such as textbooks, workbooks, activity packages, and the like. Due to the multitude of these educational materials, it is important to know how effective they are in helping teachers pursue desired instructional strategies. Content analysis can determine which materials are appropriate and of a high quality.

Content analysis is a general assessment technique by which complex materials such as textbooks can be reduced to simpler terms; for instance, categorization of content, level of mental functioning, readability scores, and so on. We need to specify what features of the textbook make it appropriate for particular instructional processes. For example, if variety of corrective procedures or alternative forms of content presentation are desired instructional procedures, we would assess the degree to which the instructional materials are suitable for such features. Other features may include the nature of topic organization, the kinds and amount of practice exercises, the availability of feedback and corrective means, or the availability of explicit statements of objectives.

It is also possible to assess whether the materials are feasible and practical for use by teachers or students. Do teachers need special training in order to understand the materials? What special teaching or learning problems are likely to occur with these materials?

Eash (1974) focused on four general constructs relevant to the nature and quality of many available instructional materials: objectives, organization (scope and sequence), methodology, and evaluation. Under each construct, several typical approaches or features of instructional materials are listed. For instance, under the objectives construct there are several questions to be answered "yes" or "no," such as: Are objectives stated for the use of the material? Are they general objectives, instructional objectives, and so on? At the end of each section, the evaluator is asked to use a 7-point scale to judge the overall worth of the instructional materials.

Among the other systems that analyze instructional materials are *A Source Book for the Evaluation of Instructional Material and Media* (Armstrong, 1973) and *The Social Studies Curriculum Analysis Short Form* (Kownslar, 1974).

Content analysis of instructional materials is valuable not only for selecting new materials but also for analyzing existing materials. It helps teachers determine to what extent materials can be used to implement desired instructional processes and discover deficiencies that require changes or supplementary materials in the classroom.

Techniques for Self-Evaluation

Particular emphasis is given to teachers' self-evaluation techniques in their own classrooms. Three possible instruments are the teacher self-evaluation checklist, the student self-report checklist, and the questionnaire for analyzing instructional and learning materials.

The *teacher's self-evaluation checklist* (Figure 4) includes 45 statements that describe a teacher's activities in the classroom regarding feedback-corrective procedures (statements 1-12), instructional cues (statements 13-32), and the facilitation of student involvement in learning (statements 33-45). Many teachers assess the strengths and weaknesses of their instruction at the end of a lesson or at the end of a school day. This checklist can help teachers evaluate their instructional and management procedures.

A teacher may find that he or she has not included all of the suggested instructional procedures in each lesson. Nevertheless, over a period of time most positive and desired behaviors should occur. Ultimately, a teacher should expect to get more "yes" responses to positive (+) statements and more "no" responses to negative (−) statements.

Figure 4. Teacher's Self-Evaluation Checklist

Directions: The following statements describe some activities and characteristics of classroom instruction that are believed to be useful in improving the learning of most students. Please read each statement and indicate whether it reflects your activities or feelings in your class today. The answer for each statement is either Yes or No.

In my class today:

		YES	NO
+	1. I let students know how well their learning is progressing.		
+	2. I let students know what they still have to learn to achieve mastery or correct their mistakes.		
−	3. I did not state explicitly enough the mastery criteria students need to achieve.		
+	4. I referred students to alternative instructional materials to correct test items they missed (or correct misunderstandings).		
+	5. I formed group activities to encourage students to help each other master the materials taught.		

YES   NO

— 6. I did not stress what the students accomplished; I mainly emphasized what they have not accomplished.

+ 7. I used different mastery criteria for different students in the class.

+ 8. I assigned additional homework assignments to students who have not reached the mastery criteria.

— 9. My reactions to students' responses were not satisfactory; I simply stated whether they responded correctly or incorrectly.

+ 10. I repeated students' correct responses to ensure that each student heard.

+ 11. I explained again to the whole class the test items that most students did not answer correctly.

+ 12. I invited a few students for an afternoon session to explain their mistakes.

+ 13. I started the lesson by stating the specific objectives of the lesson.

+ 14. I wrote an outline of the lesson on the blackboard.

+ 15. I related the new ideas taught in class to earlier content.

— 16. The sequence of activities within the lesson seemed difficult to most students.

— 17. I encouraged students to practice exercises that stress mainly lower levels of thinking.

* 18. Practice exercises were very similar to each other.

— 19. I did not provide sufficient verbal explanations to accompany demonstrations.

— 20. I did not use enough cues of different natures to adapt to the needs of different students.

+ 21. I watched carefully students' (or a representative group of students') facial expressions to see if I needed to give further cues or explanations.

+ 22. I felt my use of cues was spontaneous.

— 23. I had difficulties using the audio-visual aids.

+ 24. I encouraged students to ask questions before I moved to a new topic.

+ 25. I gave a brief summary of the major ideas (or skills) at the end of the lesson.

* This may be a positive procedure in some instances, but not regularly.

YES   NO

+ 26. At the end of the lesson, I restated the objectives of the lesson.
+ 27. Most of my questions were answered correctly by the students.
− 28. Most of the higher level questions were not answered correctly.
+ 29. I realized what kind of cues are helpful to weak students and which are helpful to better students.
+ 30. After I asked a particular student a question, I gave the child enough time to respond.
+ 31. I emphasized the importance of a topic (concept or skill) by explicitly stating its importance.
+ 32. Before I moved to teach a new concept (topic or skill) I indicated the transition to the students.
 * 33. I called on students to respond in a particular order (for example, alphabetically or by seating arrangement).
+ 34. Most of the students participated in the discussions.
+ 35. I prepared instructional and learning aids before the lesson began.
+ 36. I moved about in the classroom.
+ 37. I changed the pattern of instruction used in previous lessons.
+ 38. I reinforced verbally or otherwise the attention and participation of the class as a *whole.*
− 39. I was unable to use examples of a high level of interest for the students.
+ 40. I realized that a few students were unable to participate actively; I asked them to come and talk to me after the lesson.
− 41. I wasted too much time on organizational issues.
− 42. I faced more discipline problems than usual — it seems to be due to a lack of clarity.
+ 43. I used *individual* rewards or reinforcement (verbal or other kinds) for good or attentive behaviors.
+ 44. I changed the seating arrangement of the students.
+ 45. I asked a student to repeat responses or explanations given by another student.

* This may be a positive procedure in some instances, but not regularly.

The *student self-report checklist* (Figure 5) includes 25 statements describing student activities and thoughts during a class. The statements are concerned with student behaviors in relation to feedback-corrective procedures (1-8), instructional cues (9-18), and the degree of their involvement in learning (19-25). Instruction is effective in facilitating student learning if students understand what they have to do and if they take an active part in the process. Therefore, to evaluate the effectiveness of our instruction, it is not enough to assess whether we have used the most desirable instructional procedures. We must look at students as the mirror for our efforts, and to learn whether instructional activities were clear and helpful and whether they evoked desired behaviors.

The student self-report checklist is relatively short and may be used at the end of each lesson or two lessons. A teacher also may decide to shorten the checklist to include fewer statements from each section. We suggest choosing different statements and changing their order so as to avoid pat responses from the students each time the checklist is used. Ask for anonymity to ensure frankness and openness in students' responses.

Teachers can easily summarize the results of their students' responses by counting the number of "favorable" or "unfavorable" responses to each item. Favorable responses are composed of "Yes" answers to positive statements and "No" answers to negative statements. Unfavorable responses are composed of "No" answers to positive statements and "Yes" answers to negative statements.

The negative and positive signs should not appear on the checklists given to students.

Figure 5. Student Self-Report Checklist

Directions: The following statements describe student activities and thoughts during classroom lessons. Please read each statement and check (√) YES if it applies to your thoughts or actions during class today. Check (√) NO next to those statements that do not apply. Do not write your name on the paper. We wish to use your responses and those of your classmates to help improve classroom instruction and learning.

During class today:

		YES	NO
+ 1.	I tried to figure out exactly where I went wrong in a problem.		
+ 2.	The teacher's remark clarified the source of my mistake.		

YES   NO

+ 3. I asked for help from another student in order to correct a mistake I made.
− 4. I was reluctant to look for help from the textbook suggested by the teacher in order to correct a mistake.
+ 5. I know precisely what I am expected to achieve in the coming test.
− 6. I didn't know for sure how well I progressed in my learning.
+ 7. I asked the teacher a question when I didn't understand something.
− 8. I didn't know what to do when I answered a problem incorrectly.
+ 9. I understood how the topics covered in class were related to previous topics we learned.
− 10. I had some troubles understanding the objectives of today's lesson.
+ 11. It was clear to me what I had to do to solve the practice exercises.
+ 12. I felt the demonstrations provided to me in class were very helpful.
+ 13. I could easily identify and follow the sequence of the lesson.
− 14. I thought the teacher moved along too quickly.
− 15. The use of pictures would have helped me understand better the ideas taught in class today.
+ 16. I tried to visualize in my head the problems we discussed.
+ 17. I was able to separate the important issues from the details.
+ 18. The use of different kinds of explanations to the same problem was extremely helpful to me.
− 19. I didn't raise my hand at all in class today.
− 20. It was hard to start working.
+ 21. I paid attention almost the whole class period.
+ 22. I wrote down some things (notes) about what we learned.
− 23. I thought about something besides the lesson during class.
+ 24. I participated in class activities although they weren't very interesting.
− 25. I started to lose my concentration toward the end of class.

The *questionnaire for analyzing instructional and learning materials* (Figure 6) is designed to help teachers or administrators decide whether new materials or existing ones can facilitate instructional procedures. It also may help teachers decide whether they can ask some students to work on their own using the materials while teachers give individual attention and guidance to other students. Analysis of the materials helps teachers prepare in advance additional instructional aids or procedures.

Figure 6. Questionnaire for Analyzing Instructional and Learning Materials

---

Directions: The following questions refer to selected aspects of instructional and learning materials. Answer each of the questions to help you decide whether or not to use selected materials in your own classroom.

Performance Criteria:

1. Are the criteria for student performance specified? Yes No
2. If criteria are specified, what is the typical level required?
   (a) 80% — 100% correct answers
   (b) 60% — 80% correct answers
   (c) less than 60% correct answers
3. Are there indications or recommendations for various types of criteria for different students in the class? Yes No

Feedback Information:

4. Are there recommended evaluation procedures for students? Yes No
5. Are the evaluation procedures or instruments compatible with the instructional objectives? Yes No
6. Do the materials include recommendations (or suggestions) for when to collect feedback information? Yes No

Correctives:

7. Are there recommendations for corrective measures of student misunderstandings? Yes No
8. Are alternative explanations available for the basic or important instructional objectives? Yes No
9. Are references to additional textbooks for further explanations specified? Yes No
10. Is there a list or a description of the necessary prerequisites for the major instructional objectives? Yes No

Instructional Cues:

11. Do the materials include a statement of instructional objectives? Yes No

12. Is the statement of objectives clear and detailed to be helpful for teachers or students? Yes No
13. Do the materials include paragraphs that relate new topics to previous topics? Yes No
14. Are questions inserted in the materials at the end of a topic or subtopic? Yes No
15. Are these questions mainly factual (lower level questions)? Yes No
16. Are answers provided to the questions posed in the materials? Yes No
17. Do the materials include figures, pictures, or demonstrations? Yes No
18. Are the figures, pictures, or demonstrations clear and helpful? Yes No
19. Do the materials include practice exercises? Yes No
20. Are the practice exercises homogeneous (similar to each other)? Yes No
21. Are there recommendations for different ways of introducing a topic for students of different achievement levels? Yes No
22. Is the sequence of instruction proposed in the materials appropriate? Yes No
23. What is the nature of the sequence?
    (a) From easy to more difficult tasks
    (b) Chronological sequence
    (c) Category organization (according to subtopics)
    (d) From abstract to concrete
    (e) Others _____
24. Are there brief summaries or reviews of the major ideas at the end of a topic or chapter? Yes No
25. Are there suggestions for using instructional games or other learning aids? Yes No
26. Can the materials be used effectively by a teacher with no special training? Yes No
27. The materials can be used effectively by most students.
    (a) Strongly agree
    (b) Moderately agree
    (c) Agree
    (d) Disagree
    (e) Strongly disagree
28. The materials will help you implement the classroom processes suggested in this book.
    (a) Strongly agree
    (b) Moderately agree
    (c) Agree
    (d) Disagree
    (e) Strongly disagree

5. Implications for Teaching and Learning

The social and technological changes in modern societies have brought about great and rapid changes in the nature and functions of school systems throughout the world. The demand for mass education and the dissatisfaction with schools have challenged educators to seek ways of adapting education to the needs of all students. If schools are to achieve the major goals of education in modern society, teachers must learn to work in different ways to improve the learning of a wide range of students. Parents and students also need to accommodate themselves to the demands, expectations, and opportunities that schools can and should provide.

Teachers and educational researchers have sought new solutions and new ways of studying the processes involved in school learning. In the past, researchers tended to stress the effects of relatively stable characteristics of students or teachers. For example, much work has been done to develop intelligence and aptitude tests and to examine the degree to which student characteristics predict scholastic achievement. Teachers and administrators have used these tests to account for difficulties in learning. The effect was to weed out those students whose test scores were regarded as too low (without regard for the causes of low scores). Similarly, much research has been carried out on the relationship between teachers' characteristics (personality, training, verbal ability, and so on) and the effectiveness of their instruction. This approach suggested that effective teaching could be expected only from a limited group of teachers.

A lot of research on school learning has emphasized associational relationships between a set of variables (usually unalterable variables) and student achievement on a desired set of learning outcomes. These relationships indicate the predictive value of variables and may suggest possible causal relationships among them. But the emphasis on unalterable characteristics of teachers and students greatly limits the relevance of such research as a basis for improving learning. There is no doubt that students and teachers differ in their cultural background, personality, intelligence, and aptitudes. But if these are highly stable characteristics that cannot be readily altered, we can do little with such research findings.

More recently, researchers have begun to focus on the alterable characteristics of students and teachers and their interrelations in the classroom. Greater attention is now given to causal relationships between student achievement and interest in learning, the teacher's use of time, and instructional strategies. To establish casual links, researchers carry out experiments using varying instructional processes and examine their differential effects on student learning. The goal of such research is to determine which approaches have the greatest direct effect on learning processes and products. These studies, when carried out in classroom learning situations, identify instructional and learning conditions that have maximal effect on students' achievement, interests, and attitudes. Moving from the study of a small number of relatively stable characteristics of teachers and students to a much larger set of alterable and interactive processes enables teachers and researchers to identify some of the essential conditions for learning and instruction.

We have provided evidence about teaching and learning processes that can be used to meet the new needs and demands of the educational system. Management and instructional processes, learning materials, and activities that are carefully developed and used widely can enhance students' ability to attend, to focus on the relevant aspects of ideas being taught, to master the objectives set for them, to retain knowledge, and ultimately to learn how to learn. These classroom processes help facilitate students' attitudes about learning and schools, and about themselves. If such procedures and experiences are not adequately planned or implemented, we limit students' ability to take an active role in the process of learning, to achieve desired learning goals, and to view education as a desired and attainable challenge.

Doyle and Ponder (1977) suggest that teachers are most likely to accept advice for improving their teaching when it meets three criteria. The advice must be operational and decribe actual teacher behaviors; it must be consistent with the teacher's own role definition; and it must be cost-effective in terms of time and energy. The instructional and management procedures emphasized in this book meet these three criteria. They are operational, based on classroom research; as such, they are consistent with teachers' practice and view of their role. Yet they allow enough variety and freedom for teachers to choose and use them idiosyncratically so as to optimally match their self-role definition. They do not require special means, techniques, or instruments. They are mainly based on existing means in a typical school and classroom. They are also rooted in the teacher's knowledge, sensitivity, intuition, and interest in his or her work.

Thus, not too much additional energy is required to implement an effective instructional procedure. Its cost, when judged in terms of improving student learning and increasing teacher satisfaction, is self-evident.

The Question of Individual Differences

A major implication of our approach to learning and instruction is concerned with the concept of educational practices and the question of individual differences. There is a prevailing view among many educators that not all students can learn what schools and teachers desire to teach or achieve. Consequently, individual differences provide a ready-made excuse, and the blame for students' inability to learn is placed on the students' genetic or environmental background. Only on rare occasions do we hear teachers explaining students' inability to learn as a result of the way they were taught.

Individual differences among students, differences over which the school has no control, do exist. Yet these individual differences are not necessarily reflected in student learning outcomes. On the contrary, individual differences should and must be reflected in the processes of learning and instruction. According to Bloom (1976), if teachers or curriculum developers can identify the cognitive prerequisites (skills and knowledge) and affective entry characteristics (attitude, interest, self-concept), and ensure that all students sufficiently possess them, it would be possible to reduce individual differences in student achievement by up to 75 percent. That is, most students would achieve roughly the same high level usually attained by only the best students.

Studies and large-scale projects using the mastery learning strategy prove that this is indeed possible. Moreover, the experience accumulated from the mastery learning strategy demonstrates that the improved achievement of lower ability students (under mastery learning conditions) does not come at the expense of the achievement of higher ability students. Mastery learning conditions seem to bring the achievement level of lower ability students up to the level of their higher ability classmates, rather than dragging down the achievement of the higher ability students. There are also indications that mastery learning conditions can reduce individual differences not only in achievement, but also in the rates of learning and forgetting. The major instructional procedure that aids in achieving these results is adequate feedback-corrective procedures in relation to a predetermined performance standard.

A thorough selection of instructional cues and an adequate and sensitive use of alternative patterns of instruction also further reduce individual differences in student learning outcomes. Varied cues, an appropriate sequence of instruction, the timing of transition from one activity to the next, a rationally based and sensitive definition of the performance standard, and a careful use of reinforcement and rewards are some effective methods for matching or adapting learning opportunities to existing differences among students. Adapting instructional and learning processes to the needs of individual students ensures that individual differences will not condition the level of achievement of most students.

Such adaptation does not necessarily require the implementation of individualized instructional programs, which sometimes necessitates major changes in the physical organization of the class or the school. It is feasible to adjust existing instructional and learning processes to students' backgrounds, abilities, interests, and learning styles within the framework of group instruction. A teacher can use a variety of spontaneous or planned methods that are appropriate to different individuals in a whole classroom setting. A teacher may also decide occasionally to use different instructional settings such as small group activities or individual seatwork. These are effective as long as the basic principles of effective learning and instruction are followed.

Anyone can develop the ability to properly adjust to individual differences. Our success as teachers depends on several factors—continuous experiences with relevant behaviors, willingness to change and correct procedures through formal or informal self-evaluation of behaviors, positive and sensitive acceptance of students' responses to classroom processes, confidence in our ability to teach, and our expectations and beliefs in the potential of school and schooling for all students.

Teachers' expectations are evident in inferential judgments about student behaviors. Many teachers begin a course or a new term expecting that about a third of their students will adequately learn what they have to teach. They expect another third to fail or just "get by." They expect the remainder to learn a good deal of what is taught, but not enough to be regarded as "good students." These expectations are sometimes supported by school policies and grading practices that are transmitted to the students through grading procedures. Research evidence in both naturalistic and experimental studies have shown that teacher expectations indeed affect how much students learn (Braun, 1976; Brophy and Good, 1974). How can we explain such a phenomenon? Why and under what conditions can teachers' expectations influence who will learn and how much will be learned?

Ordinarily, expectations result from observed behaviors rather than cause them. Yet, if expectations are inflexible and rigid, they are capable also of causing future behaviors and performance. This self-fulfilling prophecy occurs when an expectation or prediction, initially false, initiates a series of events that cause the original expectation to come about. Thus, when a teacher's expectation acts as a self-fulfilling prophecy, it functions as a cause of student behavior rather than as a result of observed behavior. Since expectations affect our perceptions as well as our behaviors, teachers may develop, consciously or unconsciously, a tendency to notice evidence of failure in students while disregarding students' success or their potential to succeed. Such a mechanism of selective perception of teachers is dangerous since it is likely to reinforce low expectations.

Research evidence suggests that teachers sometimes tend to prefer students from higher social class homes, to overestimate their ability and to develop great hopes for their academic performance. Researchers also noticed that when this is so, teachers tend to make more frequent and facilitating patterns of interaction in the class with the preferred students. In contrast, there is evidence (Brophy and Good, 1974) that the most effective teachers have realistic and correct expectations concerning their students. They are neither overly romantic nor painfully discouraged. They tend to recognize real differences among students, but they use this information to plan their instruction in order to optimally assist all students in the classroom. They do not merely label students or use differences among students as an excuse for failing to teach them adequately.

Adapting to the needs of the individual student is extremely challenging to teachers and educators. It is essential, therefore, that teachers and educators realize such adaptation is feasible. This will enable them to develop adequate instructional procedures as well as realistic expectations and a flexible approach to teaching. Rigid or false attitudes or expectations result in less effective instruction. It is also likely to reinforce the view that only some students are capable of achieving—a view that has been an educational restraint for a long time.

Classroom Climate

One may feel that analyzing classroom processes separately may cause us to lose the picture and characteristics of the class as a whole. Indeed, there are global properties of classes that determine the quality of life in the classroom.

We often think of a classroom as the context or environment in which instruction and learning take place. This encompasses the conditions, forces, and external stimuli that impinge on the students and the teacher. According to Dewey (1916), environment is "the particular medium in which an individual exists which leads him to see and feel one thing rather than another . . . it strengthens some beliefs and weakens others, it gradually produces in him a certain system of behavior . . . the environment consists of those conditions that promote or hinder, stimulate or inhibit the characteristics or activities of a human being." A classroom is, then, a particular kind of environment in which physical, psychological, social, and intellectual stimuli set the conditions for the behaviors of students and teachers. Those conditions give a class its particular character.

Anyone who has ever taught knows that a classroom possesses a distinct atmosphere or *climate*. Some classes are more or less organized; some classes manifest tension and anxiety; others communicate a great degree of freedom for individual students. Instructional and learning climate can be thought of as the generalized attitudes, feelings, and actions that prevail in a class.

Five major dimensions of classroom climate are direct consequences of the instructional procedures and principles emphasized in this book: academic orientation; teacher directiveness; structure; cooperation and affiliation (social reactions); and support and concern for individuality.

1. Academic orientation—the focus and emphasis given in a classroom to academic activities. The principles and procedures we have suggested lead to classes that have a high level of academic orientation, that is, classrooms in which most activities are centered around the accomplishment of academic objectives.

Teachers in such classes maintain a strong academic focus by using the time allocated for instructional purposes in a way that enables them to spend the least amount of time on nonacademic activities. They organize classroom processes in different ways to ensure an optimal degree of student involvement in academic activities. High levels of academic orientation may be inferred from the frequency of homework assignments and from the kinds of activities students are encouraged to be engaged in outside the classroom periods.

Classrooms of low or moderate academic orientation spend a considerable amount of time on additional stimulations, such as games, stories, or discussions that are not directly relevant to the learning objectives. Discipline and organizational problems use up time originally allocated for instruction. Homework assignments are optional and academically oriented out-of-class activities are not encouraged.

2. Teacher directiveness—the nature of authority or leadership in the class. Classrooms in which activities are controlled and guided by teachers have relatively strong teacher directiveness. The teacher is perceived as a strong leader who directs student activities and leaves relatively little freedom for students to select their learning tasks, their seats, or their learning methods. The teacher decides on the objectives to be mastered and the performance standards, and monitors student learning, supervises individual students as well as groups, reinforces activities, and provides rewards.

Typically, a teacher maintains control by judging what shall be done, who shall do it, and when.

Classes in which students take a major part in decisions may be viewed as having weak teacher directiveness. In these classes students have freedom to move about, talk to each other, and work with one another. They also accept the responsibility for their own performance and achievement.

The procedures we emphasize encourage the creation of classrooms where the teacher assumes dominant leadership. This may sound to some as creating a formal, cold, nonpermissive, and authoritative climate. This is clearly not the case. Although students may have little freedom in decisions, they have much freedom in helping the teacher structure effective instruction. By communicating to the teacher their difficulties, by responding to the teacher's questions or requests, the students play a crucial role in the decision-making process. We have emphasized the central role of students in shaping and affecting the process of instruction by serving as a mirror to the teacher. This divides the responsibility for effective learning and instruction between the students and the teacher. Thus, in some aspects of classroom life, students' freedom is quite limited. Yet, in other aspects, students are active partners in the instructional process orchestrated by the teacher.

3. Structure—the nature of classroom organization. In highly structured classrooms, there is a clear and careful plan of well organized activities. Teachers in highly structured classrooms can easily relate previous ideas or activities to present and future ones. Transition from one activity to the next is smooth and rationally based. Similarly, teachers in highly structured classes manage to channel diverse activities that occur simultaneously. Rules are explicitly stated and clearly understood by students. Students usually know when to learn, what to learn, and why.

Classrooms in which activities are not well organized and the lesson plans unclear are low structured classes. In low structured classes, it is difficult to infer the rationale behind the sequence of activities, nor does the sequence offer orientation for the teacher and the students. Rules for conduct in the classroom are frequently changed and students may become confused about their expected roles and about ideas they need to learn.

One need not practice rigidity or inflexibility to establish structured instructional situations. Structure refers mainly to systematic patterns of instruction and classroom management. It refers to planned activities, but these may also be accompanied by spontaneous and intuitive instructional cues. Structure does not connote rigidity; it implies a framework within which much flexibility is feasible and desirable.

4. Cooperation and affiliation—the interpersonal relationships among students in the class. Classrooms in which students come to know each other and help each other master personal and group goals are considered high in cooperation and affiliation. Often, a high level of cooperation and affiliation in the class is inferred from the ways in which students resolve academic and social problems that occur in class. In contrast, there are classrooms in which much time and energy is spent on competition and hostility among peers. Students often compete for the teacher's attention, for grades and rewards, or for leadership in the class. In such classes, the potential for a student's isolation is high; the formation of small cliques is likely; and a lack of solidarity and mutual concern is strongly felt.

Effective classroom processes, their implicit values and explicit manifestations, encourage a great deal of cooperation and affiliation among students. For example, the definition of a performance standard expected of all students in the class gives them a common goal and a common challenge to meet as a group. Corrective procedures form the framework within which close acquaintance, cooperation, and mutual concern are enhanced. Highly succeeding students, those who perform faster and better, become models rather than leaders or stars. Student evaluation becomes a less threatening experience. It is not a process in which a student's progress is judged in relation to his or her classmates (norm reference). Rather, it is based on a criterion reference judgment—the degree to which students have reached the criterion set for them.

We do not foresee a class as a place in which social pressures, tension, competition, or quarrels are totally nonexistent. They are not feasible or desired, however. The class is a place in which students learn to live together for a relatively long period of time. It provides experiences likely to be found outside the classroom and in adult life. It may sometimes resemble experiences within a large family. Yet, the conditions of learning created in the classroom provide students with social skills and personal confidence which will enable them to resolve social conflicts or pressures in a frank, open, and sensitive manner.

5. Support and concern for individuality—the extent to which differences among students in the classroom are accepted, respected, and adequately treated. In classes where strong support and concern for individuality exist, teachers manage to feel or diagnose individual differences and to use them as a guide in their instructional plans and decisions. Similarly, students become aware of and tolerant toward differences among each other. In classrooms where weak support and concern for individuality is communicated, teachers either are not aware enough of real differences among students or do not use these differences appropriately in their instructional processes. Verbal or nonverbal emphasis only of individual differences becomes destructive if it is accompanied by a negative attitude toward such differences and helps to develop unreal and rigid expectations of teachers and students.

In previous chapters we focused mainly on instructional procedures that take into account differences among students in their pace of learning, style, and ability to learn. Yet, there are many more potential aspects to differences among students such as their interests, motivations, desires, aspirations, moods, and needs. Thus, we may refer to the "group personality" of a classroom when we speak of the class as a social unit, but we need to realize that a group personality is compounded by the personality of each individual in the class.

Our basic thesis behind effective classroom processes regards the individual student as a mirror for the teacher's decisions and behaviors and fosters the creation of a climate offering a high degree of support and concern for individuality. The development of an atmosphere in which differences among students are respected requires concern for the student's background, performance, and needs; different patterns of instruction; a variety of instructional cues; monitoring performance and progress; and various kinds of rewards adapted to student needs.

Typically, teachers' behaviors and attitudes serve as a model for students. Students learn to respect each other, to appreciate differences among themselves, to be realistic, and to learn to use their differences in a way that satisfies the needs of the group as well as the personal needs of individuals. They spend their time and energy constructively and thus create an extremely humane atmosphere.

The classroom provides a continual source of actual and potential stimuli, demands, and consequences. Students do not behave in a vacuum. They respond in a particular environmental context that, in part, determines their behaviors. In addition, their attitudes, expectations, feelings, and needs determine, to some extent, the nature of the forces that exist in their environment. Yet the teacher and the instructional processes are mainly responsible for developing classroom climate. Teachers structure and restructure learning situations that determine the nature and power of the forces and demands in the classroom. This produces different kinds of emotional, social, and intellectual climates that have different effects on student achievement.

In this book we have concentrated on a few instructional and learning processes believed to have the greatest effect on the improvement of learning and teaching. These processes and the variety of ways they can be implemented may bring a new reality to the quality of life in the classroom—a reality that enables students to meet the needs and demands of society. Teachers and educators must be willing to give up some of their traditional and comfortable beliefs about effective instruction and life in the classroom.

There is larger number of variables and instructional processes that have smaller effects on learning and instruction. We must constantly search for additional variables that may have equal or greater effects on educational outcomes than those discussed here. Clearly, there is much need for further research. The quest for the improvement of education and student learning is never-ending.

Annotated Bibliography

Articles written during the past two decades that emphasize the strengths of the procedures explained in this book.

Anderson, Lorin, W. "An Empirical Investigation of Individual Differences in Time to Learn." *Journal of Educational Psychology* 68 (1976): 223-233.

An investigation of the magnitude and stability of individual differences in the amount of time required to achieve a criterion level of performance. The study hypothesized that students who are provided with additional time and help to attain criterion levels in the early units of a three-unit sequence spend approximately the same amount of time-on-task to attain the criterion level on a final unit as students who attain the criterion on the early units with no extra time and help. Ninety eighth-grade students taken from a middle-class population participated in the study. They were randomly assigned either to a mastery learning class, in which they were helped to attain an 85 percent mastery standard, or to one of two non-mastery classes. Students in all three groups learned a three-unit sequence of programmed material in matrix arithmetic. All students were given the programmed text and a unit formative test. They were instructed to write on their booklet the time they began working. When they finished the booklet, they again wrote down the time and picked up the formative test. They wrote the time they began work on the formative test, when they completed the test, and when they finished it. All three classes proceeded in the same manner up to this point. In the mastery learning class, students who did not attain the 85 percent criterion level were asked to complete review exercises that were keyed to each item of the test. The students recorded their review time. They were then given a review test and once again asked to record the time they began and the time they finished. Every student in the mastery class was able to attain an 85 percent criterion level with no more than two review-corrective periods. The students in the nonmastery groups did not receive extra help and time for corrective purposes. Two measures of learning time were used in the study: elapsed time and time-on-task. *Elapsed* time refers to the amount of clock time that passed between the beginning and end of the actual learning time (with testing time not included). This was calculated for each student, based on his or her recording. *Time-on-task* refers to the time during which the student was actively involved in learning. The measurement of time-on-task included two components: overt (observable) on-task behaviors and covert (nonobservable) on-task behaviors. The first component was measured through a classroom observation instrument. The second component was measured by using the stimulated recall technique developed by Bloom (1953). The major results of the study were as follows: (1) For the first unit in the sequence, students in the nonmastery classes and in the mastery class who attained the criterion level in the original amount of elapsed time were similar in the amount of time-on-task required. In contrast, students in the mastery learning class who were able to attain the desired criterion only with the allotment of additional amounts of elapsed time and help required approximately 66 percent more on-task time than their classmates who attained mastery in the original amount of elapsed time. In the second unit, students in the mastery class who needed more time and help to reach the criterion required approximately 30 percent more time-on-task on the average than their mastery learning classmates. In the third unit, the group of students who needed more help to reach the criterion required only five percent more time-on-task than did their mastery learning classmates. (2) In the first unit, students who attained the criterion level spent significantly less elapsed time than students who needed more time and help. The magnitude of this difference decreased in the second unit. In the third unit, no significant differences were observed between the groups. (3) In the first unit no significant differences were found in the percent of time actually devoted to learning (time-on-task) between students who reached the criterion level and students who failed to reach the level. In units 2 and 3, the difference between these two groups of students and the actual magnitude of the difference increased over the two units. The results of the study imply that the amount of time-on-task required to reach a pre-set criterion can be altered by an effective review-corrective procedure. In addition, the results show that a relatively heterogeneous group of students can become homogeneous in the amount of time-on-task they require to learn a particular task after mastering a series of prerequisite tasks.

Ausubel, David P. "The Use of Advance Organizers in the Learning and Retention of Meaningful Verbal Material." *Journal of Educational Psychology* 51 (1960): 267-272.

A study of the degree to which the learning and retention of unfamiliar but meaningful verbal material can be facilitated by advance introduction of relevant subsuming concepts—organizers. The organizers in the present study were introduced prior to the learning of unfamiliar material. The sample consisted of 120 seniors. The experiment was performed during regular class hours. The learning material was a specially prepared 2,500-word passage dealing with the metallurgical properties of plain carbon steel. This topic was chosen because it was generally unfamiliar to undergraduates yet sufficiently elementary to be comprehensible and interesting. In addition, two introductory passages were constructed. The *experimental* introductory passage contained background material of a much higher level of abstraction, generality, and inclusiveness than the latter passage. The introductory passage was designed to serve as an organizing or anchoring focus for the subsequent material, and was carefully designed so as not to contain specific information that would aid in answering the criterion test. The *control* introductory passage, on the other hand, consisted of historically relevant background; a type of introductory material traditionally included in textbooks. The control introductory passage contained no conceptual material that could serve as a framework for organizing the ideas of the learning passage. Subjects were assigned to one of the two treatment groups—experimental or control. Both groups studied the steel passage for 35 minutes and took the criterion test three days later. The results demonstrated that the differences in retention between the experimental and control groups were significant. Subjects exposed to the experimental introductory passage scored higher than their control group counterparts.

Block, James H., and Tierney, Michael L. "An Exploration of Two Correction Procedures Used in Mastery Learning Approaches to Instruction." *Journal of Educational Psychology* 66 (1974): 962-967.

This study explored the impact of the correction procedure on student learning as a necessary stage in an instructional strategy. The study also investigated the effectiveness of two types of corrective procedures that are known to be part of two versions of the mastery learning strategy. One is Keller's Personalized System of Instruction and the second is Bloom's Approach to Learning for Mastery Strategy. In Keller's approach, the corrective procedures require students to return to the original materials and methods for the segment upon which they are having learning problems, while in the Bloom approach students use supplementary instructional materials and methods to learn problematic subject matter in different ways. The research involved 44 college students who were randomly assigned to three instructional treatment groups. The first treatment, the control treatment, was the traditional lecture/discussion approach. Subjects attended 50-minute lectures three times a week during the quarter and read six required books. The second treatment, the redirected study treatment, used the traditional approach plus a Keller-type correction procedure. Once every two weeks students in this group received a diagnostic-progress or formative test on the readings and lectures for the preceding two-week period. These tests were returned to each student with an indication of which items the student had answered correctly, the correct answers to missed items, and a prescription for learning the unlearned material. The prescription directed the students to restudy and review the original reading materials and lecture notes. The third treatment group, the small study treatment, used the traditional approach plus a Bloom-type correction procedure. Students in this group were given the same tests biweekly, but they had their test results returned during cooperative small-study sessions. In these sessions, each student was asked to select one of the questions he or she had answered correctly and to explain the specific answer. The other students were encouraged to ask questions. This procedure was followed until all of the items on the test had been discussed. Within each treatment group, half of the students were pretested with the achievement measure and the attitude scale and the remaining subjects were not pretested. Accordingly, the design for the study was a 2 x 3 factorial design. The results indicate that students who received correction periodically throughout the course did not learn more than students who received no correction when learning was manifest in terms of students' knowledge of the material taught, their final course grade, and their attitude toward the subject matter. This was true regardless of the type of correctives used. But if learning was measured in terms of the students' ability to *apply* the learned material, students who received correction did learn more than students who received no correction, provided that correction was accomplished by sending the student to different instruction (small-group study). The study suggested that application of the course material could be significantly improved if students used a correction procedure that exposed them to *supplementary* instructional methods and materials rather than those that required them to review and practice the original materials.

Brophy, Jere E., and Good, Thomas L. "Teachers' Communication of Differential Expectations for Children's Classroom Performance: Some Behavioral Data." *Journal of Educational Psychology* 61 (1970): 365-374.

This study investigated the processes by which teachers communicate different performance expectations to students. The authors were interested in exploring teacher expectations, which are assumed to function as self-fulfilling prophecies, in the administration of a criterion achievement test. The study was carried out in four first-grade classrooms. The four teachers involved were asked to rank the students in their classes in the order of achievement. These ratings were then used as the measure of teachers' expectations for students' performance. In each class, six students (three boys and three girls) high on the teacher's list and six students (three boys and three girls) low on the teacher's list were selected for observations. In order to focus on differential treatment of different students, the study used an observation system addressed to dyadic contacts between the teacher and the individual student, while other teacher behaviors were ignored. The type of interactions coded included recitation, reading, and answers to teachers' questions; in addition, other types of interactions initiated by the students were observed. One major feature that was coded consistently was whether the interaction was initiated by the teacher or by the student. Coders also noted the quality of the students' responses and the evaluative nature of feedback given by the teachers. In addition to the coding of dyadic interactions, Students' hand raising was tallied as a measure of their tendency to seek response opportunities. The observations were made on four separate days in each of the four classes, and extended for an entire morning or an entire afternoon. The results were as follows: (1) Students for whom the teacher held high expectations raised their hands more frequently and initiated more procedural and work-related interactions than did students for whom the teacher held low expectations. (2) There was a tendency for the teachers to initiate more contacts with the students for whom they held low expectations than with the students for whom they held high expectations. However, these were *criticisms* rather than work-related contacts. (3) Students for whom the teacher held high expectations produced more correct answers in the reading groups and achieved higher average scores on the end-of-year standard test than did students for whom the teacher held low expectations. (4) The teachers were more persistent in eliciting responses from the highs by giving them more than one opportunity to respond. The teachers failed to give feedback only 3.3 percent of the time when reacting to highs, compared to 14.7 percent of the time when reacting to lows. (5) Teachers had more disapproval contacts with boys than girls. The findings of the study indicated that teachers did, in fact, communicate different performance expectations to different children through their classroom behavior, and the nature of this different treatment encouraged students to begin to respond in ways that could confirm teacher expectancies.

DeYung, Alan John. "Classroom Climate and Class Success: A Class Study at the University Level." *The Journal of Educational Research* 70 (1977): 252-257.

This study hypothesized that greater congruence between the real and ideal climate of a classroom would be reflected in increased student appreciation and satisfaction for the course and its content. In contrast to more traditional student evaluation of classrooms, which looked at teacher quality, this study chose to assess classroom climate through the entire social intellectual atmosphere. A modified version of the Classroom Environment Scale, developed by Moos and Trickett, was used to assess the real classroom climate as perceived by students. It contained 90 true-false items on nine subscales: involvement, affiliation, teacher-support, task orientation, competition, order and organization, rule clarity, teacher control, and innovation. In addition, a short version for rapid assessment of ideal and expected climate was used. The course under consideration for this study was a required two-unit sociology-social psychology section for junior and senior education majors. The study entailed two phases. Initially, the real and ideal versions of the classroom environment scales were given to the students in Class A approximately halfway through one academic quarter. Subsequently, the discrepancies between real and ideal scores were identified. This information was used to restructure course content and operation for the subsequent class in social psychology and education (Class B). Since attendance in the course was not mandatory for either class, a careful attendance record was kept for both quarters. In addition, students reported data on overall course appreciation, class content, class functioning, and teacher quality. The results were as follows: (1) A discrepancy between ideal and real-perceived climate was established in Class A. For example, while students wanted appreciable amounts of involvement and affiliation, they actually perceived almost none of these features in the class. The only areas of congruence were competition, order and organization, and teacher control. (2) The social climate desired by Class B (after changes in course content and operation were carried out) was almost identical to that desired by Class A. However, differences were established between the two classes in the two real climate profiles. Real subscales scores for Class B on such dimensions as involvement, affiliation, support and rule clarity, which the investigator tried to change, were all closer to the ideal climate than were the real scores in Class A. (3) Attendance for Class A was smaller than attendance for Class B. Also, students in Class B felt that their class was better organized, more interesting, and that the discussions were of a higher intellectual quality. The research suggests that it is quite possible to change social climate and that a more ideal climate was linked to students' satisfaction and motivation to attend class.

Duchastel, Philippe C., and Brown, Bobby R. "Incidental and Relevant Learning with Instructional Objectives." *Journal of Educational Psychology* 66 (1974): 481-485.

This research examined the role of students' knowledge of learning objectives. The authors hypothesized that through knowledge of objectives students can decide which material to concentrate on and which to pay less attention to. A sample of 58 college students volunteered to participate in the study. The course was organized around a set of 24 objectives developed from an examination of the instructional reading passage. All objectives were very specific and stated what the student would be expected to do once he or she finished studying the text. The post-test was developed so as to reflect directly the instructional objectives. Subjects were randomly assigned to two treatment groups. The first group received half of the objectives that had been randomly selected from the full list. The second group received no objectives and were instructed to learn everything in the text. The subjects had a maximum of 30 minutes in which to study the passage. During the learning task, the subjects were permitted to review any section of the text at their discretion. Each subject decided when he or she was satisfied, wrote down the exact time, and received the post-test. Post-test directions indicated to the subjects that they should try to answer all items. The results were as follows: (1) The group receiving half of the objectives performed better than the group receiving none of the objectives on the subtest that was referenced to the partial list of objectives received by the group. The group receiving half of the objectives performed less well than the group receiving none of the objectives on the subtest that was referenced to the set of objectives *not* received by the group. This indicates that relevant learning was enhanced by the availability of objectives, whereas incidental learning was depressed by the availability of objectives. (2) No difference in the amount of time each student spent studying the text was established between the group receiving half of the objectives and the group receiving none of the objectives. This research supports the hypothesis that knowledge of very specific objectives facilitates learning by focusing the learning effort on relevant material and simultaneously detracting attention from incidental material. The results, however, are directly generalizable only to the knowledge category of learning.

Field, Ronald L., and Okey, James R. "The Effects of Formative Evaluation and Remediation on Mastery of Intellectual Skills." *The Journal of Educational Research* 75 (1975): 253-255.

The major purpose of this study was to examine the relative effectiveness of two remediation (corrective) procedures: learning or relearning prerequisite skills and repeated practice of the learned task. The subjects involved in the study were 90 eighth-grade general science students in four different classes taught by one instructor. Random assignment of the subjects produced three treatment groups of 30 subjects each. All classroom activities during the study were directed by the regular classroom teacher. During the experiment, each student studied a block of self-instructional material on identifying variables, constructing graphs, and interpreting graphs. The instructional materials were designed to teach each of the tasks in a learning hierarchy, consisting of a terminal task and 13 subordinate skills. All students were presented a tape-slide program on constructing a table of data. At the end of the presentation the students took a diagnostic test covering the objectives of the instruction. The results of the diagnostic test were used to indicate which skills each subject had not acquired from the main-line instruction. Subjects in Group 1 who were not successful in a particular test item received additional *instruction* on objectives *prerequisite* to those in the main-line instruction. Group 2 subjects received additional *practice* items *similar* to those in main-line instruction. Subjects in Group 3 received no additional instruction. All remedial activities used paper-and-pencil materials on which the subjects responded to a problem and received immediate feedback. This instruction-diagnostic test-remedial activity sequence was repeated three times during the study and occupied a total of six class periods. Following the third remedial period, all subjects were tested on the criterion measure, which consisted of 13 items covering the terminal task and 12 of the subordinate skills. The results of the study demonstrate a significant difference in scores attained by students who received remediation compared with scores attained by students who received no remediation. A significant difference in achievement was found between the two remediation groups. The study demonstrates that an alternative form of instruction, such as additional instruction on prerequisite skills, produces a more significant improvement in achievement than does using additional practice items as remediation. These results imply that remediating learning errors is more effective through practice and mastery of the necessary prerequisite skills for a particular task.

Frase, Lawrence T. "Effect of Question Location, Pacing, and Mode Upon Retention of Prose Material." *Journal of Educational Psychology* 59 (1968): 244-249.

The research explored the effect of question location, question pacing, location of relevant content, and question mode on the retention of relevant and incidental learning outcomes. Subjects were 128 introductory psychology students. A 2000-word passage, which was divided into 20 paragraphs of 10 lines each, served as the stimulus material. Each paragraph included two multiple-choice items, one relating to the first half of the paragraph and one relating to the second. For half the subjects, the questions relating to the first part of the paragraph were placed before or after the paragraph. For the remaining subjects, the questions related to the second part of the paragraphs and were also placed before or after the paragraphs. The questions the subjects saw while reading the material were called relevant questions. The other half of the questions were called incidental. The criterion retention test consisted of both relevant and incidental items. The subjects were randomly assigned experimental materials and instructed to read each page, not to review or look back at any page after reading it, and to answer the questions when they were encountered. When they completed the reading task, the subjects received the final test. This study employed a design in which factors were (a) question location —before or after the paragraph; (b) question pacing—after every 10, 20, 40, or 50 sentences (one question after each 10 sentences, two questions after 20 sentences); (c) content location—question-relevant material located in the first or second part of each paragraph; and (d) question mode —multiple-choice or constructed response. The results were: (1) Questions facilitated retention more when they were placed after the prose passage. (2) Retention of the relevant information was significantly higher than retention of the incidental information. (3) The advantage of questions that were placed after the paragraph increased as the number and frequency of the questions increased. Conversely, the disadvantage of placing questions in front of the paragraphs was strongest when the questions occurred most frequently. (4) Regardless of pacing or location of questions, higher incidental retention was achieved if the incidental material followed the relevant material. (5) No differences between multiple-choice and constructed response items were established.

Glynn, Shawn M., and DiVesta, Francis J. "Outline and Hierarchical Organization as Aids for Study and Retrieval." *Journal of Educational Psychology* 69 (1977): 89-95.

This study examined the effects of variations in the logical sequencing of paragraphs in a text. These effects were studied in terms of the recall of specific and general facts and of reconstructions of material learned. The subjects were 120 undergraduate students who were awarded points toward their course grades for participating. The text material was generated from 15 hierarchically structured topics. Two versions of the text were employed to manipulate sequence. In one, a text was sequenced logically by ordering the 15 paragraphs to reflect the hierarchy of the topic structure. In the other variation, the sequence was scrambled by random ordering of the independent paragraphs within the passage. Thus, the paragraphs of the two texts were identical, but the degree to which the topics followed a logical progression was varied. The structural outline was used as an advance structural outline and as a retrieval structural outline. These enabled the subjects to identify the topics, their sequence, and their hierarchical relationships. The learning task was administered to 15 groups, each comprised of eight subjects. Each student in a group was randomly assigned to one of the experimental conditions. The experimental session lasted from 45 to 60 minutes, at the end of which each student was tested on his or her recall of the learned material. The results were as follows: (1) The provision of an advanced structural outline led to a greater proportion of specific facts being recalled by the subjects than when this aid was not provided. Also, the proportion of specific reproductive facts recalled by the subjects was significantly greater than the proportion of the general reproductive facts in both the presence and the absence of an advanced structural outline. (2) The presence of a retrieval structural outline significantly affected recall when paragraphs were scrambled, but did not significantly affect recall when paragraphs were sequenced logically. In addition, performance on productive recall under the logical paragraph sequence condition was higher than performance under the scrambled paragraph sequence condition in the absence of the retrieval structural outline.

Good, Thomas L., and Beckerman, Merrill M. "Time on Task: A Naturalistic Study in Sixth-Grade Classrooms." *The Elementary School Journal* 78 (1978): 193-201.

The study investigated whether student involvement was different for high, middle, and low achievers. It also explored whether certain types of classroom activities were associated with higher or lower levels of student involvement. Two different types of schools were selected, one in which students represented a wide range of socioeconomic status, and one in which students came from working-class or lower middle-class homes. In both schools, all sixth-grade classrooms were included in the study, three classrooms in each school. Classroom instruction in both schools was primarily self-contained. Six coders collected 14 hours of observational data in each class. Four major types of information were collected regarding: (a) the instructional setting (whole class or small group, with or without teacher supervision); (b) the type of activity students were engaged in (writing, waiting for the teacher, walking, talking); (c) the subject matter under study (mathematics, reading, art, science); and (d) the level of task involvement (definitely involved, definitely not involved, misbehavior, indeterminate). The coders looked at each student in each class in turn, determined the student setting, activity, and level of attention. At the end of the study, teachers were asked to assign each student to one of three achievement groups (high, middle, low) on the basis of overall achievement. The authors report a high level of observation reliability (85 percent or better). The major findings were: (1) High achievers spend more time on task (are more involved) than low achievers. (The gap between high achievers and low achievers becomes greater in subject areas that are traditionally emphasized—76 percent of high achieving students vs. 64 percent of low achieving students). (2) Student involvement seems to vary with the subject being taught. Students were observed to be more involved during mathematics and spelling. In addition, the instructional setting seems to have an important influence on student involvement. Students' involvement is highest when they are studying in small groups (86 percent of the students were definitely involved) or in a large group with teacher supervision (80 percent of the students were definitely involved). In contrast, student involvement drops during individual activities. In a large classroom setting where the teacher typically lectures and students listen, only 60 percent of the students were definitely involved.

Greabell, Leon C. "The Effect of Stimuli Input on the Acquisition of Introductory Geometric Concepts by Elementary School Children." *School Science and Mathematics LXVIII* (1978): 320-326.

The study was designed to determine if planned exposure to a greater number of stimuli in the process of learning will affect student achievement in an introductory course in geometry. In this study there were several references made to increase stimuli. Stimuli were defined by nine categories (based on the Functional Analysis of Classroom Tasks); each represented a sensory component and a cognitional component. Three types of sensory subcomponents were used—visual, auditory, and tactile. The cognitional component also had three subcomponents—concrete, representative, and abstract. The nine kinds of stimuli reflect, therefore, each pair of the two sets of subcomponents. For example, visual and concrete stimuli emphasize viewing an object around which the learning is centered. Auditory and concrete reflect the learning of the real object. Tactile makes use of physical feeling of a representation of an object, thing, or idea around which the learning is centered. Two groups were defined for the purpose of the study—a low stimuli group (LSG) and a high stimuli group (HSG). For the LSG ($N = 51$) a series of nine lessons in geometry was designed using a widely-used children's mathematics text as a basis for planning. The lessons contained no additional forms of stimuli other than those recommended by the text, that is, mainly visual-abstract and abstract-abstract. For the HSG ($N = 57$) the same lesson plans were used, but additional stimuli were systematically incorporated into each lesson as defined by the nine categories. Auditory-concrete and tactile-abstract were not referenced even once in the lessons of the HSG. The students ($N = 108$) selected for the study represent a random school population of seven-, eight-, and nine-year-olds. No student had formal instruction in geometry before the experiment. The students were randomly assigned to self-contained classrooms in two elementary schools and studied in 11 groups, five of which were LSG and six HSG. Over a two-week period each group was given approximately 45 minutes of instruction per day on geometry; on the tenth day each group was given the post-test. The results of the study indicated that students in the HSG scored higher than students in the LSG. Systematically planning and increasing stimuli in geometry did show an effect on achievement.

Hops, Hyman, and Cobb, Joseph A. "Initial Investigations into Academic Survival—Skill Training, Direct Instruction, and First-Grade Achievement." *Journal of Educational Psychology* 66 (1974): 548-553.

This study explored the relative effects of training in academic survival skills vs. direct instruction with the use of an individualized curriculum on reading achievement. Survival skills are defined as specific classroom behaviors (for example, attentiveness to a teacher, participation in classroom discussion) that are not academic responses per se but are the necessary basis for academic behaviors. The study was conducted in four first-grade classrooms, which were randomly assigned to three experimental conditions: one class served as control; another class received direct individualized instruction (DI); and two classes received group survival skill training (GSS). Student behaviors were observed during all reading periods for five consecutive days. Using an interactive coding system developed by the authors, the observers recorded the behavior of each student for a minimum of two consecutive eight-second intervals before going on to the next student. After all students had been coded once, the process was repeated. Thus, the behavior of each student was sampled about the same number of times during each session. Four skills were observed: attending, working, volunteering, and looking around. To compute a student's survival-skill level, the frequency of looking around was subtracted from the summed frequencies of attending, volunteering, and working. This figure was divided by the total frequency of all behaviors and represented the proportion of academic survival-skill behaviors for each student. The experimental manipulation occurred in the regular classroom setting and lasted for 20 school days. The primary focus was to alter teacher behaviors in order to enhance favorable academic and survival behaviors in the students. In the group survival skill program (GSS), teachers were trained to use modeling, daily feedback, cueing, and so on. In particular, teachers were trained in how to pair group-nonsocial reinforcement with individual and group-social reinforcement, vicarious reinforcement, shaping procedures, close monitoring, and the withdrawal of nonsocial reinforcement by gradually increasing the criterion for such reinforcement. The approach used in the direct instruction (DI) of reading was based on the assumption that reading can be taught in a programmatic fashion by individualizing the curriculum. The reading tests were analyzed into a hierarchy of subskills. The teacher had to identify the entering behaviors or particular subskill levels of each student, who was then taught the next task in the hierarchy. Each student was tested to determine whether he or she had mastered a subskill before proceeding to the next. The teacher in the control class was provided with a graduate student who acted as a teacher aide during the study. The student and the teacher were given no specific instructions. Two achievement tests were used: The Gates MacGinitie Primary A and the Gates-MacGinitie Reading Readiness tests. These were administered both prior to and six weeks after the termination of the formal intervention procedures. Gain scores for both survival skills and mean achievement were used as the dependent variables of the study. The major findings of the study follow: (1) Classrooms that received the group survival-skill training made greater gain in survival-skill behaviors than those that did not receive the training. (2) Students who received direct programmatic instruction in reading increased significantly their achievement level but not their survival-skill behavior. (3) Students in the survival-skill training program demonstrated greater gains in achievement and survival skills than did students of the control class. (4) Scores in reading achievement were increased both by direct instruction in reading and also by survival-skill training. The study suggests that even with an effective curriculum, a teacher may need help in classroom management for increasing students' survival-skill behaviors such as attentiveness, work, and volunteered participation in discussions.

Howe, M. J. A., and Singer, Linda. "Presentation Variables and Students' Activities in Meaningful Learning." *British Journal of Educational Psychology* 45 (1975): 52-61.

Two experiments were conducted to measure what effect different procedures students use to learn a new prose passage have on subsequent recall. In the first experiment, three procedures were investigated: reading a descriptive prose passage, copying the passage, and summarizing (taking notes) while reading. These experimental conditions were designed to test the efficacy of active involvement in learning. The copying condition was designed to involve the student in some of the activities involved in summarizing, but summarizing involves the student in active processing and coding behaviors. The 86 subjects in the first experiment were first-year undergraduate students who attended two successive weekly sessions. In the first session, each subject received experimental instructions together with the prose passage. The three experimental groups were given different instructions. Group One was told to spend 10 minutes reading the text and rereading it if time allowed. Group Two was told to use the same time copying the passage, as far as possible, word by word. Subjects in Group Three were told to make a summary of each paragraph in the prose passage. All students were warned that they might subsequently be asked questions about the subject matter. After 10 minutes, the test for retention of the passage content was administered. Contrary to expectations, the performance of the students who simply read the passage was superior on both the immediate test and the long-term test, although on the long-term test the difference between the reading and summarizing groups was not significant. The authors explained that students in the reading group could perform better because their learning conditions allowed maximum freedom to use whatever strategies, procedures, and habits the students found valuable in coping with a new task. Since the findings differed markedly from another study by the same authors, in which subjects did not read the passage but listened to it, a second experiment was carried out in which both presentation conditions and subjects' activities were manipulated. The purpose was, then, to ascertain how the different combinations of these two variables influence performance. In experiment two, some subjects read the passage, some listened to it at dictation speed, and others listened to repeated auditory presentation at a normal speaking rate. Within each of these three groups, some students were required to record the passage by copying it in writing, and others made no overt response. The second experiment included 96 undergraduate students who were allocated at random to the different experimental conditions. The results revealed that with written presentation, subjects who simply read the passage performed better than those who were also required to record the information by copying it. With auditory presentation at dictation speed, no differences existed between those who recorded the passage and those who simply read it. Among those who listened to the passage at normal speed, students who merely listened obtained subsequent recall scores twice as high as students who had to record the information. The findings show, therefore, that students who were allowed to distribute their attention as they wanted performed better by not having to submit to the constraints necessitated by having to record the information. Also, when subjects were already constrained in the manner in which they directed their attention, the requirement to record the passage did not impose any further constraint.

Hughes, David D. "An Experimental Investigation of the Effects of Pupil Responding and Teacher Reacting on Pupil Achievement. Experiment III: Teacher Reaction." *American Educational Research Journal* 1 (1973): 21-37.

This study was part of a series of experimental studies of teacher effectiveness in the classroom. In each study the researcher gave classes lessons that had been planned in detail and memorized, thus minimizing extraneous teacher behavior variables. All the information to be provided to students, its sequence, the wording of teachers' reactions to student responses, and so forth, were predetermined. The specific purpose of the experiment was to study the effect of teacher reactions to students' overt responses on student achievement. Subjects were Form II students (roughly equivalent to U.S. seventh grade) from 13 classrooms in five intermediate schools. The experimental lessons dealt with three exotic game animals of New Zealand that are not part of the regular science program. In order to study the effects of positive teacher reactions on pupil achievement, two treatment groups were used—reacting and nonreacting. The students in the reacting group received frequent praise for giving correct answers ("Very good," followed by the correct answer). They received support for giving incorrect answers ("Not a bad effort, but . . .," followed by the correct answer); and they were urged or mildly reproved when the situation warranted ("Haven't you any idea?"). The students in the nonreacting group generally received little more than a statement of the correct answer. The results of the study revealed that the two treatment groups differed significantly on their mean residual achievement score, indicating a higher residual score for the reacting group compared to the nonreacting group. Moreover, teachers' reactions affected students' scores on both the post-test items relevant to the questions they responded to and the post-test items not relevant to the questions. The findings indicate that this positive/mildly negative teacher reaction to student responses, where appropriate, facilitates student achievement more than minimal teacher reactions.

Johnson, David; Johnson, Roger T.; Johnson, Jeanette; and Anderson, Douglas. "Effects of Cooperative Versus Individualized Instruction on Students' Prosocial Behavior, Attitudes Toward Learning, and Achievement." *Journal of Educational Psychology* 68 (1976): 446-452.

This study explored the relative effects of cooperative and individualistic goal structures on three types of learning outcomes: student prosocial behavior (altruism and the ability to take the affective perspective of others), attitudes toward learning, and achievement. The study hypothesized that the way teachers structure classroom learning determines the way students interact with each other and with the teacher; this, in turn, affects the cognitive and affective outcomes of instruction. The authors conceptualized cooperative and individualized goal structures. Under a cooperative goal structure, when one student achieves his or her goal, all students achieve their goals. Under an individualized goal structure, the goal achievement of one student is unrelated to the goal achievement of other students. These two ways of structuring learning lead to different interaction patterns and are expected to promote different learning outcomes. The subjects of the study, fifth-graders, learned language arts for a 17-day period. Students were randomly assigned to one of the two treatment groups, the individualized condition or the cooperative condition. Cooperation was operationally defined as instructing students to study together as a group, completing one assignment sheet per group, seeking help from each other, and individually receiving teacher praise. During the study, students participated in no other cooperative academic learning experiences. Also, daily observations were made to test and verify that student behavior was in fact appropriate to the assigned condition. The observation data indicated that students did in fact study in their assigned condition. At the end of the study, students were given the criteria measures. The results indicated that cooperative interaction with peers promotes altruistic behavior of students compared with studying individually. The results of the study also provide some evidence indicating that cooperative learning experiences facilitate intrinsic motivation to learn, while individualized learning experiences may facilitate extrinsic motivation to learn. The findings also support the contention that cooperation is positively correlated with feelings of acceptance and support by teachers and peers, as well as with liking for peers. Finally, the results of this study demonstrated that higher daily achievement results from cooperative learning, but no differences exist between cooperative and individualized conditions on a review test given individually. Yet, when the review test was taken cooperatively by the students in the cooperative condition and individually by the students on the individualized condition, the cooperative group did better.

Kulhavy, Raymond W.; Yekovich, Frank R.; and Dyer, James W. "Feedback and Response Confidence." *Journal of Educational Psychology* 68 (1976): 522-528.

This study explored the corrective nature of feedback in relation to students' confidence in their behavior. The subjects were 67 undergraduate volunteers. They were randomly assigned to each feedback condition—present and absent. The experimental test was a modified version of a 30-frame program, "The Structure and Function of the Human Eye," which was previously used in studies. The frames averaged 82 words in length, and each frame included a five-item multiple-choice question related to its content. The scale on which the subjects rated their confidence in the correctness of an answer was located at the bottom of the page following the question. The scale contained five points ranging from 1 (low confidence) to 5 (sure of answer). The post-test consisted of the same questions seen in the program. Subjects in the feedback condition were given a Trainer-Tester Response Card, which was keyed to the correct responses in the program. Subjects made their program responses by erasing the circle they felt corresponded to the correct frame response. When the circle was erased, the subjects saw either a T if their choice was correct or another letter if the response was incorrect. Subjects participated in small groups. In the two conditions, subjects were told to read each frame carefully, answer the question, rate their confidence on the correctness of the selected response, and record their frame time. Students in the feedback condition were also given instructions on how to use the Trainer-Tester Response Card and were told to erase alternative selections for each item until they located the correct choice identified by T. They were also asked to record the total time they spent on the feedback procedure. The immediate post-test was administered following the program with no time limit on completing the test. One week later, the delayed test was administered. The results were as follows. (1) Students who received feedback had superior performance compared to students who received no feedback. However, this success cannot be attributed to either longer study times nor to less frequent errors during learning. (2) Students who received feedback were more likely to remember their correct program responses on a later test than were students who received no feedback. (3) For high-confidence correct answers, feedback helped the students remember that the response was correct, at least on an immediate post-test. Also, when subjects received feedback following a high-confidence error, they showed a marked tendency to be able to correct themselves on an immediate test and to a lesser degree on a delayed measure. (4) Error responses required significantly more time for the subjects to complete the feedback procedure. Also, at the higher levels of confidence ratings (4 and 5), feedback time was longer for errors and shorter for correct answers. This study favors the contention that the effects of feedback are largely determined by the students' perception of their original response. Feedback, according to these results, is most successful when it follows a response in which the subject has high confidence. When confidence is high in an error response, feedback acts as a strong corrective device. Alternately, when the response is high-confidence and correct, seeing feedback increased the probability of repeating the correct answer.

Lahaderne, Henriette, M. "Attitudinal and Intellectual Correlates of Attention: A Study of Four Classrooms." *Journal of Educational Psychology* 59 (1968): 320-324.

This study examined whether children's attentiveness in class is related to their attitudes toward school and the teacher on the one hand, and to achievement and ability on the other. The subjects were 125 students (62 boys and 63 girls) enrolled in four sixth-grade classrooms in a predominantly white, working-class suburb. Their classroom behavior was observed over a three-month period, in 37 hours of observation with approximately nine hours spent in each of the four classrooms. Questionnaires were administered to the students and background data, such as IQ and achievement test scores, were obtained from school records. The observational scheme was a modified version of the Jackson-Hudgins observation schedule. The observer recorded the state of each student's attention, according to four classifications: (1) "+" if the student was attentive—attending to the subject and activity designated by the teacher, such as reading or writing; (2) "−" if the student was clearly inattentive —not attending to the area of focus or the prescribed activity; (3) "?" if the observer was uncertain whether or not the student was attentive; (4) "0" if the student's attention was not observable. Interobserver reliability ranged from 83 percent to 100 percent in trial observations. The student's attitudes toward four aspects of school life—the curriculum, teacher, peers, and the school—were measured by a 47-item multiple-choice questionnaire. Students' attitudes toward their teacher and schoolwork were measured by a 37-item questionnaire. The achievement and ability tests were derived from the Scott-Foresman Basic Reading Test, the Stanford Achievement Test, and the Kuhlmann-Anderson Intelligence Test. The main findings follow. (1) The correlations between attention and measures of achievement were significant. They ranged between −.53 for inattentive students to +.51 for attentive students. The student who paid attention gained the most from the instruction, while the student who was inattentive was not apt to achieve academically. (2) The partical correlation coefficient between achievement and attention, with IQ held constant, ranged from .26 to .31 and seemed to depend on the type of achievement test. (3) For neither boys nor girls were feelings toward the school and the teacher related to their attention of the dominant class activity. (4) Low correlations were found between students' attitudes and their achievement test scores and IQ. The author discusses possible explanations for the lack of a relationship between the way students felt about school and their attentiveness in class. One possible explanation is that the constraints imposed on students to be attentive were so strong that attitudes could not influence behavior. The author also discusses possible explanations for the relatively strong relationship between intelligence measures and student attentiveness. A usual classroom situation in which the teacher directs the curriculum to the class average may strengthen the relationship between intelligence and attention. This implies, according to the author, that a curvilinear rather than a linear relation may exist between attention and level of instruction.

Measel, Wes, and Mood, Darlene W. "Teacher Verbal Behavior and Teacher and Pupil Thinking in Elementary School." *The Journal of Educational Research* 66 (1972): 99-102.

This study explored the relationships between modes of teacher verbal influence and the sophistication of pupil thinking. It also explored the relationships between the levels of teacher and pupil thinking in the classroom. The more specific purpose of the study was to determine if the degree of abstraction observed in the verbal behavior of children was related to the level of thinking observed in the teacher's verbal behavior or to the teacher's mode of behavior. A sample of 15 female second-grade teachers participated in the experiment. The 399 students in the 15 classrooms composed the student sample, which included 214 boys and 185 girls. Each teacher was observed for approximately 12 hours. In order to provide an adequate sampling of all interactions in the various subject matter areas, observations were divided between mornings and afternoons. Observations were recorded every 3 seconds, showing both the category of interaction and, when appropriate, the level of thinking inherent in either the pupil's or the teacher's verbalization. The basic data collection instrument was Flanders' 10-category system of classroom interaction analysis, which designates seven categories of teacher talk, two of pupil talk, and one of silence. A system of levels of thinking was added to the following four categories of the Flanders' system: teacher lectures, teacher questions, pupil responds, and pupil initiates. This system includes three hierarchical levels: Level A represents statements or questions dealing with memory, previously learned material, or simple description; Level B includes statements or questions that differentiate between phenomena, grouping activities, and simple explanations; and Level C represents statements or questions that require inference, derivation by reasoning, concluding from evidence, telling why, and constructing cause and effect statements. The results reveal that teachers and pupils function largely at the lower levels of thinking. For example, teacher questions took up 11.2 percent of the total interaction, and of that, 83 percent were at the lowest level of thinking. Similar high proportions of pupil talk were at the lowest level of thinking. Almost all of the higher level statements and questions by teachers were taken directly from various teacher guides; virtually no use of the higher mental functions was observed during teacher-initiated class discussions. The study demonstrates a relationship between the level of thinking inherent in the teacher's verbal behavior and that of his or her students. When teachers function at higher levels of thinking, their students also tend to function at those levels.

Page, Ellis B. "Teacher Comments and Student Performance: A Seventy-four Classroom Experiment in School Motivation." *Journal of Educational Psychology* 49 (1958): 173-181.

The study investigated two questions: Do teacher comments cause a significant improvement in student performance? If comments have an effect, which comments have more than others, and what are the conditions conducive to such effect? Seventy-four teachers, randomly selected from among secondary teachers of three districts, participated, and each teacher randomly chose one of his or her classes for study. The classes represented all secondary grades (7 through 12), most of the subject-matter areas, and consisted of 2,139 students. The teachers first administered an objective test that would ordinarily come next in the course of study. The tests were marked in the usual way with a numerical score and a letter grade of A, B, C, D, or F. Then the teachers randomly assigned each paper to one of three groups: no comment, free comment, or specified comment. No-comment students received nothing else. Free-comment students received whatever comment the teacher wanted to make. Specified-comment students all received comments designated in advance for each letter grade: A, "Excellent! Keep it up"; B, "Good work; keep at it"; C, "Perhaps try to do still better?"; D, "Let's bring this up"; and F, "Let's raise this grade." The test papers were then returned to the students. The effects of the comments were judged by the scores the students received on the next test. The main findings were as follows. (1) Free-comment students achieved higher scores than specified-comment students, and specified-comment students did better than no-comment students. All differences were significant except those between free-comment and specified-comment students. (2) When comment effect was compared among 12 different schools, no significant differences were revealed. (3) There was an indication that comment effects were similar among junior high and senior high students. (4) Although teachers believed their better students were much more responsive to teacher comments than were poorer students, the experiment did not support this belief.

Reynolds, James H., and Glaser, Robert. "Effects of Repetition and Spaced Review Upon Retention of a Complex Learning Task." *Journal of Educational Psychology* LV (1964): 297-308.

This research evaluated the effect of repetition and spaced review on retention of a complex and meaningful learning task in two studies. In these studies an attempt was made to explore these effects on conditions approximating classroom learning. The researchers used programmed instruction built of 1,280 frames covering ten topics in biology. Within this program, the sixth topic—a 115-frame sequence—was selected for experimental variations. Using the original 115-frame sequence as a standard, two new sequences were written that taught the same material but differed from the original form in the frequency the technical terms were repeated. One contained 50 percent less repetitions and one contained 50 percent more repetitions, as compared to the original form. By inserting any one of the three experimental sequences into the larger program at Topic 6, the amount of repetition of the experimental material was varied while the presentation of prior and subsequent learning material was kept constant. To provide for space review, two short sections were written. They were inserted after Topic 7 and Topic 8. According to the design, one review condition contained the same number of repetitions of the terms as the standard form, but spaced them over several topics rather than presenting them intact. A second review condition had 50 percent more repetitions than the standard form and was equivalent in number of repetitions to the experimental condition, but they were also distributed over topics rather than massed. A total of 75 junior-high school students and 58 eighth-graders participated in the first and the second experiments, respectively. Criteria measures of recall and recognition of the terms were used to assess retention. The results were as follows. (1) Repetition differences had only a limited effect on retention of programmed materials, and even this limited effect disappeared over a relatively short period of time. (2) Spacing of review sequences had a facilitating effect on retention of material learned in a programmed sequence.

Royer, James M., and Cable, Glenn W. "Illustrations, Analogies and Facilitative Transfer in Prose Learning." *Journal of Educational Psychology* 68 1976): 205-209.

The present research explored the effectiveness of using illustrations and physical analogies on students' ability to transfer learned material. Based on assumptions about knowledge structures, the researchers tested their hypothesis, which indicated that the following two conditions in the learning process of a two-passage sequence facilitates positive transfer: (1) the initial passage to which the subjects are exposed establishes a knowledge bridge between known information and new information contained in the next passage; and (2) the next (target) passage is diffcult to comprehend. Four versions of the first passage were constructed differently and could be characterized as abstract with illustrations, abstract with analogies, concrete, and unembellished abstract. An unrelated passage was also included to serve as a control. The first four passages were concerned with heat flow or electrical conductivity, while the control passage was concerned with an unrelated topic. The concrete version contained as many concrete referents as possible. The abstract version was largely devoid of concrete referents and contained neither physical analogies nor illustrations. The abstract-with-analogies version was very similar in style to the regular abstract passage, but differed in content since it contained the physical analogies which added real-world phenomena. The abstract-with-illustrations passage was similar in content to the abstract passage, except that it was accompanied by drawings. Illustrations were used with the abstract rather than with the concrete passage since the authors believed that illustrations are effective only in situations where the text to be learned is diffcult to comprehend. Five groups (N = 80) received five different initial passages. All the groups received an abstract passage, which was concerned with a topic different from the initial passage, as the second passage. The prediction was that the concrete group, the abstract-with-analogies group, and the abstract-with-illustrations group would recall significantly more from the second passage than would the control and abstract groups. Also, it was hypothesized that the former three groups would not differ from each other in recall. The results of the study provided substantial support for the predictions. It is possible to construct a knowledge bridge between familiar and unfamiliar information with the use of an analogy between learned principles and a familar real-world event or by providing illustrations within an abstract passage. Both enable students to better comprehend difficult-to-understand material contained in an initial abstract passage, and facilitate the learning of a second passage.

Surber, John R., and Anderson, Richard C. "Delay-Retention Effect in Natural Classroom Settings." *Journal of Educational Psychology* 67 (1975): 170-173.

This experiment investigated the effect of feedback timing on student learning in a situation approximating a normal classroom. The sample consisted of 144 high school students, who participated in groups in their regular classes. Four treatment groups were formed—two received instruction prior to an initial test and two received no instruction. One of the instruction groups and one of the no-instruction groups received feedback immediately following the initial test on Day 1 of the experiment. The remaining two groups received feedback on Day 2. Of two control groups that received no feedback, one received instruction and took the initial test on Day 1 and the retention test on Day 7; the other took the test on Day 1 and Day 7, receiving neither instruction nor feedback. The form of feedback the students received was identical to the initial test, except the correct answers were underlined. Instructions for the initial test stressed that students should respond only if they were sure of an answer and make no wild guesses. Instructions for the feedback stated that the students should study the questions and answers carefully without marking the answer sheets. Instructions for the delayed test were identical to those for the initial test. The results confirmed that giving students knowledge of the correct response had a strong effect on the probability that they would correct their mistakes. The results indicated that feedback was superior to no feedback and that among the two feedback conditions, delayed feedback was better. The results favoring delayed feedback were explained with the interference-preservation theory. Over a delay interval, incorrect responses are forgotten so there is less interference in learning the correct answers from the feedback. In receiving immediate feedback, students suffer from proactive interference from the incorrect answers to which they have committed themselves. This study confirms that giving students feedback is primarily important in helping them correct their mistakes, rather than serving as reinforcement.

Traub, Ross E. "Importance of Problem Heterogeneity to Programmed Instruction." *Journal of Educational Psychology* 57 (1966): 54-60.

The main purpose of this experiment was to study problem heterogeneity as a factor in learning a complex task from a self-instructional program. The study also measured whether practice on heterogeneous and homogeneous problems is better for students of different ability levels. The four-part learning task in the study was graphical addition of integers. Three different kinds of problems were devised for inclusion in the third section of the program—heterogeneous problems, homogeneous problems, and review problems. One set of 20 problems was made heterogeneous in two respects. First, the contexts of the problems were varied; second, their answers varied in certain ways from one problem to the next. A second set of 20 problems was homogeneous. The contexts of these problems were constant and their answers were very similar. A third set of 20 problems, the review problems, was not directly related to the skills learned in the third part of the program where the problems were inserted. The four-day study was administered to 294 sixth-grade students. The three experimental groups were given the same program of instruction on the first two days, while on Day 3 each group worked on a different set of problems. The fourth part of the program served as the learning criterion. The results of the study indicated that the best performance was achieved by students who practiced with the heterogeneous problems. Practice on homogeneous problems did not differ from practice on review-unrelated problems. The findings, moreover, revealed that practice on heterogeneous problems caused students to make fewer stereotyped errors and to omit fewer responses. The effectiveness of practice with heterogeneous problems was independent of students' aptitude. The author concluded that heterogeneous problems contain more information about the task than the other kind of problems and therefore practice with these problems can produce better learning of a complex task.

Wentling, Tim L. "Mastery Versus Nonmastery Instruction with Varying Test Item Feedback Treatment." *Journal of Educational Psychology* 65 (1973): 50-58.

This study explored the outcomes of varying amounts of feedback provided to students within the framework of the mastery learning strategy as compared to a nonmastery instructional strategy. The subjects for the study were 116 male high school students who were distributed among six classes taught by three instructors. The learning material used in the study consisted of revised, published materials dealing with automobile ignition systems. Eight units contained instructions for completion, behavior objectives, textual material, and a set of review questions derived from the objectives. Three of the experimental groups were assigned to the nonmastery learning treatment, which involved measuring each student's progress at the time he finished the unit. When a student felt ready to be tested, he was given the unit achievement test and upon completion was instructed to continue with the next unit in the sequence. All tests were scored and returned to students on the day following test completion. The remaining three groups were assigned to the mastery learning treatment, which was similar to the nonmastery treatment with one exception. Rather than given a score, students were told whether or not they had reached the predetermined level of mastery (80 percent) for the unit completed. If the student met the predetermined standard, he was instructed to continue to the next unit. If he failed to meet the standard, he was instructed to return to the instructional booklet and review areas of weakness. Following review or restudy, the student was retested with a parallel form of the unit achievement test. The recycling could continue for a maximum of three times before the student was promoted to the next unit. In this experiment, three levels of specificity of feedback were used. Two of the experimental groups received no specific item feedback (no knowledge of results) from the items included in the test. Two of the remaining four groups received partial item feedback (knowledge of correctness of response) through the use of a special chemically treated answer sheet. The remaining two groups received total item feedback (knowledge of correct response) for each test item. Students in the total feedback treatment and students in the partial feedback group learned the correctness of their response. Also, if an item was answered incorrectly, students were requested to respond a second, third, or fourth time until they made the correct response. Three criterion instruments were used to measure the four dependent variables—immediate and delayed cognitive achievement, attitude toward instruction, and time used for instruction. The study lasted for five weeks and subjects attended four 70-minute class periods per week. The major findings follow. (1) Immediate cognitive achievement as well as retention of cognitive material indicate a significant advantage in favor of mastery learning over nonmastery learning, whereas in terms of attitude toward instruction no differences appeared. (2) Partial feedback treatment exceeded the other two treatments both in terms of students' immediate achievement and attitude toward instruction. More-over, the results show the total-feedback treatment as the lowest in terms of achievement. However, feedback specificity had no significant effect on retention. (3) Time spent on instruction, as reported by each student, was significantly higher in the mastery strategy compared to the non-mastery treatment. Also, the no feedback treatment was significantly more time-consuming than the total-feedback treatment, while the partial-feedback treatment did not differ significantly from either of the other two treatments. (4) A greater difference in time spent on instruction between the mastery and the nonmastery strategies existed for the total-feedback treatment over the other two treatments. (5) Low-ability students, as measured by the Otis-Lennon Mental Ability Test, spent more time on instruction than the high-ability students for the no-feedback treatment and the partial-feedback treatment, but within the total-feedback treatment high-ability students spent more time than did the low-ability students.

Wheeler, Ronald, and Ryan, Frank. "Effects of Cooperative and Competitive Classroom Environments on the Attitudes and Achievement of Elementary School Students Engaged in Social Studies Inquiry Activities." *Journal of Educational Psychology* 65 (1973): 402-407.

The central problem of this study was to ascertain to what degree elementary school students who are engaged in social studies inquiry activities differ in their achievement and attitudes as a result of participating in either a cooperative or a competitive classroom environment. Eighty-eight fifth- and sixth-graders were randomly assigned to one of the three treatment conditions: cooperative, competitive, or control. The two experimental groups were exposed to identical social studies content for 18 days. They worked on inquiry-related problems within subgroups in the cooperative condition and independently in the competitive condition. Cooperative subjects were assigned to subgroups of five or six members. Each subgroup cooperatively worked together to complete various inquiry-type activities. Each member of a subgroup was assigned a specific sub-task and, thus, made an individual contribution toward the solution of an inquiry problem. Members of the subgroups, submitting the best work-book over each five-lesson period were awarded a poster. Competitive subjects, on the other hand, worked on the same inquiry workbook, but individually rather than in subgroups. After each five-lesson period, posters were awarded to the six individual students with the best workbook. In an attempt to control the teacher personality variable, two teachers involved in the study taught both experimental treatments. Each teacher taught the cooperative group for nine lessons and the competitive group for nine lessons. The results of the study indicated no differences in achievement between the cooperative and competitive groups. This was surprising since previous research suggested that cooperative conditions positively affect student achievement. The achievement test used essentially competitive conditions and, therefore, was biased in favor of the students from the competitive treatment. The authors concluded on the basis of this analysis that meaningful evaluation of the effects of cooperative and competitive classroom environment on achievement should use alternative testing environments. The results revealed that the cooperative subjects liked social studies significantly better than the competitive subjects and that they liked sharing information, working together, and receiving group grades, rather than individual grades.

Zahorik, John A. "Classroom Feedback Behavior of Teachers." *The Journal of Educational Research* 62 (1968): 147-150.

The study explored the nature of teacher verbal feedback during the teaching-learning process. More specifically, it investigated (1) types of feedback teachers use and how frequently they use them; (2) the relationship between teacher verbal feedback and the grade level of teachers and students, the purpose of the lesson, and the type of student response. The study used recorded lessons in several elementary schools. Analysis of the transcribed lessons was carried out with a teacher-verbal feedback instrument, determining frequencies and percentages of feedback. The subjects were eight third-grade teachers and seven sixth-grade teachers and their classes. Each of the teachers taught a discussion lesson based on one issue and were asked to divide their lessons into two parts: a prereading or introductory discussion and a postreading or development discussion. The feedback instrument that analyzed the lessons contained 25 categories— 13 dealing with direct feedback and 11 describing indirect feedback. Direct feedback refers to oral remarks that convey information to students regarding the value of their behavior. Indirect feedback refers to oral questions and statements from which students can infer the value of their verbal behavior. The results concerning the general use of feedback behavior demonstrate that different types of feedback were used, but only a comparatively small number were used regularly. While the number of types of feedback individual teachers used ranged from 33 to 57, no fewer than 175 different types were displayed by all 15 teachers. Teachers most frequently (8.5 percent) repeated the student's answer approvingly and called for or gave a new topic for discussion. With the second most frequent type (8.3 percent), teachers called on the students to further develop a response. Using the third most frequent type of feedback (7.8 percent), the teacher gave simple praise and moved the lesson to a new topic. During introductory discussions, the types of feedback used more frequently contained mainly positive answer repetition, whereas feedback used frequently in development discussions mainly contained simple praise. Significant differences were found in the type of feedback used in the two grade levels. Third-grade teachers used types of feedback that contained simple praise and lesson progression. Sixth-grade teachers used positive answer repetition and solicited several answers. The author suggests that teacher verbal feedback during the interactive classroom situation was rather rigid and emphasized that the few types of feedback used regularly were less informational to students.

References

Allen, D. I. "Some Effects of Advanced Organizers and Level of Question on the Learning and Retention of Written Social Studies Material." *Journal of Educational Psychology* 61 (1970): 333-339.

Allen, M. L. *An Investigation of the Relationship Between Written Comments on Classroom Tests and Achievement In and Attitudes Toward College Mathematics.* Ph.D. dissertation, University of Virginia, 1972.

Alschuler, A.; Dacus, J.; and Atkins, S. "Discipline, Justice, and Social Literacy in the Junior High School." *Meforum* 2 (1975): 48-51.

Anderson, L. W. "Time and School Learning." Ph.D. dissertation, University of Chicago, 1973.

Anderson, L. W. "An Empirical Investigation of Individual Differences in Time to Learn." *Journal of Educational Psychology* 68 (1976): 223-233.

Anderson, L. W.; Evertson, C. M.; and Brophy, J. E. "An Experimental Study of Effective Teaching in First-Grade Reading Groups." *The Elementary School Journal* 79 (1979): 193-223.

Anderson, L. W., and Scott, C. C. "The Relationship Among Teaching Methods, Student Characteristics, and Student Involvement in Learning." *Journal of Teacher Education* 29 (1978): 52-63.

Anderson, R. C., and Biddle, W. B. "On Asking People Questions About What They are Reading." In *Psychology of Learning and Motivation.* Volume 9. Edited by G. Bower. New York: Academic Press, 1975.

Andre, T., and Kulhavy, R. W. "Category Clustering in the Free Recall of Sentences." *Psychological Reports* 29 (1971): 631-634.

Angell, G. W. "The Effect of Immediate Knowledge of Quiz Results on Final Examination Scores in Freshman Chemistry." *Journal of Educational Research* 42 (1949): 391-394.

Arlin, M. N. "Learning Rate and Learning Rate Variance Under Mastery Learning Conditions." Ph.D. dissertation, University of Chicago, 1973.

Armstrong, J. R., ed. *A Sourcebook for the Evaluation of Instructional Material and Media.* Milwaukee: University of Wisconsin, 1973.

Arnold, D. S.; Atwood, R. K.; and Rogers, V. M. "An Investigation of the Relationships Among Question Level, Response Level, and Lapse Time." *School Science and Mathematics* 73 (1973): 591-594.

Attwell, A. A.; Orpet, R. E.; and Meyers, C. E. "Kindergarten Behavior Ratings as a Predictor of Academic Achievement." *Journal of School Psychology* 6 (1967): 43-46.

Ausubel, D. P. "The Use of Advance Organizers in the Learning and Retention of Meaningful Verbal Material." *Journal of Educational Psychology* 51 (1960): 267-272.

Ausubel, D. P. *The Psychology of Meaningful Verbal Learning.* New York: Grune and Stratton, 1963.

Ausubel, D. P. *Educational Psychology: A Cognitive View.* New York: Holt, Rinehart and Winston, 1968.

Ausubel, D. P., and Fitzgerald, D. "Organizer, General Background and Antecedent Learning Variables in Sequential Verbal Learning." *Journal of Educational Psychology* 53 (1962): 243-249.

Ausubel, D. P., and Youssef, M. "The Role of Discriminability in Meaningful Parallel Learning." *Journal of Educational Psychology* 54 (1963): 331-336.

Bandura, A.; Grusec, J. E.; and Menlove, F. L. "Observational Learning as a Function of Symbolization and Incentive Set." *Child Development* 37 (1966): 500-506.

Barnes, H. L. "An Investigation of the Effects of Differential Instructional Material on Concept Acquisition and Transfer." Ph.D. dissertation, Michigan State University, 1972.

Berliner, D. "Tempus Educare." In *Research on Teaching: Concepts, Findings and Implications.* Edited by P. Peterson and H. Walberg. Berkeley, Cal.: McCutchan, 1979.

Binor, S. "The Relative Effectiveness of Mastery Learning Strategies in Second Language Acquisition." M.A. dissertation, University of Chicago, 1974.

Blaney, J. P., and McKie, D. "Knowledge of Conference Objectives and Effect Upon Learning." *Adult Education Journal* 29 (1969): 98-105.

Block, J. H. "The Effects of Various Levels of Performance on Selected Cognitive, Affective and Time Variables." Ph.D. dissertation, University of Chicago, 1970.

Block, J. H. "Student Learning and the Setting of Mastery Performance Standards." *Educational Horizons* 50 (1972): 183-191.

Block, J. H., and Anderson, L. W. *Mastery Learning in Classroom Instruction.* New York: Macmillan, 1975.

Block, J. H., and Burns, R. B. "Mastery Learning." In *Review of Research in Education.* Edited by L. S. Shulman. Itasca, Ill.: Peacock Publishers, 1976.

Block, J. H., and Tierney, M. L. "An Exploration of Two Correction Procedures Used in Mastery Learning Approaches to Instruction." *Journal of Educational Psychology* 66 (1974): 962-967.

Bloom, B. S. "Thought Processes in Lectures and Discussions." *Journal of General Education* 7 (1953): 160-169.

Bloom, B. S., ed. *Taxonomy of Educational Objectives. Handbook One: Cognitive Domain.* New York: David McKay, 1956.

Bloom, B. S. *Stability and Change in Human Characteristics.* New York: Wiley, 1964.

Bloom, B. S. "Learning for Mastery." *Evaluation Comment* 1 (1968).

Bloom, B. S. "Mastery Learning." In *Mastery Learning Theory and Practice.* Edited by J. H. Block. New York: Holt, Rinehart and Winston, 1971.

Bloom, B. S. *Human Characteristics and School Learning.* New York: McGraw-Hill, 1976.

Bloom, B. S. "Favorable Learning Conditions for All." *Teacher* 95 (1977): 22+.

Bloom, B. S. "Introduction to Mastery Learning—To the Teacher." Paper presented in Teacher Training Seminar, Chicago, 1978.

Bloom, S. *Peer and Cross-Age Tutoring in the Schools.* Washington, D.C.: National Institute of Education, 1976.

Boydell, D. "Pupil Behavior in Junior Classrooms." *British Journal of Education* 45 (1975): 122-129.

Braun, C. "Teacher Expectation: Sociopsychological Dynamics." *Review of Educational Research* 46 (1976): 185-213.

Brophy, J. E., and Evertson, C. M. *Learning from Teaching: A Developmental Perspective.* Boston: Allyn and Bacon, Inc., 1976.

Brophy, J. E., and Good, T. L. "Teachers' Communications of Differential Expectations for Children's Classroom Performance: Some Behavioral Data." *Journal of Educational Psychology* 61 (1970): 365-374.

Brophy, J. E., and Good, T. L. *Teacher-Student Relationships: Causes and Consequences.* New York: Holt, Rinehart and Winston, 1974.

Brown, J. L. "The Effects of Revealing Instructional Objectives on the Learning of Political Concepts and Attitudes in Two Role-Playing Games." Ph.D. dissertation, University of California at Los Angeles, 1970.

Brown, W. F., and Holtzman, W. H. *Survey of Study Habits and Attitudes.* New York: The Psychological Corporation, 1967.

Bruner, J. S. *Toward a Theory of Instruction.* New York: W. W. Norton & Company, Inc., 1968.

Bushnell, D., Jr.; Wrobel, P. A.; and Michaelis, M. L. "Applying 'Group' Contingencies to the Classroom Study Behavior of Preschool Children." *Journal of Applied Behavioral Analysis* 1 (1968): 56-61.

Carroll, J. B. "A Model of School Learning." *Teachers College Record* 64 (1963): 723-733.

Carroll, J. B. "On Learning from Being Told." *Educational Psychologist* 5 (1968): 4-10.

Carroll, J. B., and Spearrit, D. *A Study of a "Model of School Learning."* Cambridge, Mass.: Harvard University, Center for Research and Development on Educational Differences, 1967.

Cashen, V. M., and Leicht, K. L. "Role of the Isolation Effect on a Formal Educational Setting." *Journal of Educational Psychology* 61 (1970): 484-486.

Chadwick, B. A., and Day, R. C. "Systematic Reinforcement: Academic Performance of Underachieving Students." *Journal of Applied Behavioral Analysis* 4 (1971): 311-319.

Cobb, J. A. *Survival Skills and First-Grade Academic Achievement.* Eugene, Ore.: Center at Oregon for Research in the Behavioral Education of the Handicapped, Department of Special Education, University of Oregon, 1970.

Cobb, J. A. "Relationship of Discrete Classroom Behaviors to Fourth-Grade Academic Achievement." *Journal of Educational Psychology* 63 (1972): 74-80.

Conant, E. *Teacher and Paraprofessional Work Productivity.* Lexington, Mass.: D.C. Heath, 1973.

Corey, S. M. "The Teachers Out-Talk the Pupils." *The School Review* 48 (1940): 745-752.

Cronbach, L. J. *Educational Psychology,* 3rd ed. New York: Harcourt Brace Jovanovich, Inc., 1977.

Cronbach, L. J., and Snow, R. E. *Aptitudes and Instructional Methods.* New York: Irvington, 1976.

Currie, J. *The Principles and Practice of Common School Education.* Cincinnati: R. Clarke, 1884.

Cusick, P. *Inside High School: The Student's World.* New York: Holt, Rinehart and Winston, 1973.

Dahloff, U. *Ability Grouping, Content Validity, and Curriculum Process Analysis.* New York: Teachers College Press, 1971.

Danner, F. W. "Children's Understanding of Intersentence Organization in the Recall of Short Descriptive Passages." *Journal of Educational Psychology* 68 (1976): 174-183.

Davis, G. T. "Classroom Questions Asked by Social Studies Student Teachers." *Peabody Journal of Education* 45 (1967): 21-26.

Davis, G. T. "Effect of Precise Objectives Upon Student Achievement in Health Education." *The Journal of Experimental Education* 39 (1970): 20-23.

Dennison, P. F. "An Observation Study of a Class in an Open Plan School." M.A. thesis, University of Lancaster, 1976.

DeRose, J. "Independent Study in High School Chemistry." *Journal of Chemical Education* 47 (1970): 553-560.

Dewey, J. *Democracy and Education.* New York: The MacMillan Company, 1916.

DeYung, A. J. "Classroom Climate and Class Success: A Class Study at the University Level." *The Journal of Educational Research* 70 (1977): 252-257.

Doyle, W. "Paradigms for Research on Teacher Effectiveness." In *Review of Research on Education, Volume 5.* Edited by L. S. Schulman. Itasca, Ill.: F. E. Peacock, 1978.

Doyle, W., and Ponder, G. A. "The Practicality Ethic in Teacher Decision-Making." *Interchange* 8 (1977): 1-12.

Duchastel, P. C., and Brown, B. R. "Incidental and Relevant Learning with Instructional Objectives." *Journal of Educational Psychology* 66 (1974): 481-485.

Duncan, C. P. "Transfer After Training with Single Versus Multiple Tasks." *Journal of Experimental Psychology* 55 (1958): 63-72.

Dunkin, M. J., and Biddle, B. J. *The Study of Teaching.* New York: Holt, Rinehart and Winston, Inc., 1974.

Eash, M. J. "Instructional Materials." In *Evaluating Educational Performance: A Sourcebook of Methods, Instruments and Examples.* Edited by H. J. Walberg. Berkeley, Cal.: McCutchan Publishing Corporation, 1974.

Ebel, R. L. "Some Comments." *School Review* 75 (1967): 261-266.

Edminston, R. W., and Rhoades, B. J. "Predicting Achievement." *Journal of Educational Research* 52 (1959): 177-180.

Eisner, E. W. "Educational Objectives: Help or Hindrance." *School Review* 75 (1967): 251-282.

Ellson, D. G., and others. "Programmed Tutoring: A Teaching Aid and a Research Tool." *Reading Research Quarterly* 1 (1965).

Engel, R. S. "An Experimental Study of the Effect of Stated Behavioral Objectives on Achievement in a Unit of Instruction on Negative and Rational Base Systems of Numeration." M. A. thesis, University of Maryland, 1968.

Etter, D. C. "Adult Learner Characteristics and Instructional Objectives." Ph.D. dissertation, University of California at Los Angeles, 1969.

Ferritor, D. E.; Buckholdt, D.; Hamblin, R. L.; and Smith L. "The Non-Effects of Contingent Reinforcement for Attending Behavior on Work Accomplished." *Journal of Applied Behavioral Analysis* 5 (1972): 7-17.

Fibly, N. N.; Marliara, R. J.; and Fisher, C. W. "Allocated and Engaged Time in Different Content Area of Second and Fifth Grade Reading and Mathematics Curriculum." Paper presented at the Annual Conference of the American Educational Research Association, New York, 1977.

Field, R. L., and Okey, James R. "The Effects of Formative Evaluation and Remediation on Mastery of Intellectual Skills." *The Journal of Educational Research* 75 (1975): 253-255.

Fitzgerald, D., and Ausubel, D. P. "Cognitive Versus Affective Factors in the Learning and Retention of Controversial Material." *Journal of Educational Psychology* 54 (1963): 73-84.

Flanders, N. A. *Analyzing Classroom Behavior.* New York: Addison-Wesley, 1970.

Floyd, W. D. "An Analysis of the Oral Questioning Activity in Selected Colorado Primary Classrooms." Ph.D. dissertation, Colorado State College, 1960.

Frase, L. T. "Boundary Conditions for Mathematic Behaviors." *Review of Educational Research* 40 (1970): 337-348.

Frase, L. T. "Effect of Question Location, Pacing and Mode Upon Retention of Prose Material." *Journal of Educational Psychology* 59 (1968): 224-249.

Frase, L. T. "Paragraph Organization of Written Materials: The Influence of Conceptual Clustering Upon the Level and Organization of Recall." *Journal of Educational Psychology* 60 (1969): 394-401.

Frase, L. T. "Some Unpredicted Effects of Different Questions Upon Learning From Connected Discourse." *Journal of Educational Psychology* 59 (1968): 197-201.

Frase, L. T., and Schwartz, B. J. "Effect of Question Production and Answering on Prose Recall." *Journal of Educational Psychology* 67 (1975): 628-635.

Furst, N. F. "The Multiple Language of the Classroom." Ph.D. dissertation, Temple University, 1967.

Gage, N. L. "A Factorially Designed Experiment on Teacher Structuring, Soliciting, and Reacting." *Journal of Teacher Education* 27 (1976): 35-38.

Gage, N. L. and others. "Explorations of the Teacher's Effectiveness in Lecturing." In *Research Into Classroom Processes: Recent Developments and Next Steps.* Edited by I. Westbury and A. A. Bellack. New York: Teachers College Press, 1971.

Gagné, E. D.; Bing, S. B.; and Bing, J. R. "Combined Effect of Goal Organization and Test Expectations on Organization in Free Recall Following Learning from Text." *Journal of Educational Psychology* 69 (1977): 428-431.

Gagné, E. D., and Rothkopf, E. Z. "Text Organization and Learning Goals." *Journal of Educational Psychology* 67 (1975): 445-450.

Gagné, R. M. *The Conditions of Learning.* New York: Holt, Rinehart and Winston, 1965.

Gagné, R. M., and Basoler, O. C. "Study of Retention of Some Topics of Elementary Non-Metric Geometry." *Journal of Educational Psychology* 54 (1963): 123-131.

Gagné, R. M., and others. "Some Factors in Learning Non-Metric Geometry." Monograph of *Social Research and Child Development* 30 (1965): 42-49.

Gall, M. D. "The Use of Questions in Teaching." *Review of Educational Research* 40 (1970): 707-720.

Gallagher, J. J. "Expressive Thought by Gifted Children in the Classroom." *Elementary English* 42 (1965): 559-568.

Gardner, E. T., and Schumacher, G. M. "Effects of Contextual Organizations on Prose Retention." *Journal of Educational Psychology* 69 (1977): 146-151.

Garner, J., and Bing, M. "The Elusiveness of Pygmalion and Differences in Teacher-Pupil Contacts." *Interchange* 4 (1973): 34-42.

Gaver, D., and Richards, H. C. "Dimensions of Naturalistic Observation for the Prediction of Academic Success. *The Journal of Educational Research* 72 (1979): 123-127.

Glynn, S. M., and DiVesta, F. J. "Outline and Hierarchical Organization as Aids for Study and Retrieval." *Journal of Educational Psychology* 69 (1977): 89-95.

Goldberg, F. "Effects of Imagery on Learning Incidental Material in the Classroom." *Journal of Educational Psychology* 66 (1974): 233-237.

Good, T. L., and Beckerman, T. M. "Time on Task: A Naturalistic Study in Sixth-Grade Classrooms." *The Elementary School Journal* 78 (1978): 193-201.

Good, T. L., and Brophy, J. E. "Self-Fulfilling Prophecy." *Today's Education* 60 (1971): 52-53.

Good, T. L., and Grouws, D. A. "Teaching Effects: A Process-Product Study in Fourth-Grade Mathematics Classrooms." *Journal of Teacher Education* 28 (1977): 49-54.

Greabell, L. C. "The Effect of Stimuli Input on the Acquisition of Introductory Geometric Concepts by Elementary School Children." *School Science and Mathematics* LXXVIII (1978): 320-326.

Gump, P. V. "What's Happening in the Elementary Classroom." In *Research Into Classroom Processes.* Edited by I. Westbury and A. A. Bellack. New York: Teachers College Press, 1971.

Hake, C. *The Effects of Specified Written Comments on Achievement In and Attitude Toward Algebra and Geometry.* Ph.D. dissertation, Pennsylvania State University, 1973.

Hammer, B. "Grade Expectations, Differential Teacher Comments, and Student Performance." *Journal of Educational Psychology* 63 (1972): 454-458.

Harlow, H. F. "Learning Sets and Error Factor Theory." In *Psychology: A Study of Science, Study 1: Conceptual and Systematic Role: General Formulations, Learning and Special Processes.* Edited by S. Kock. New York: McGraw-Hill, 1959.

Harlow, H. F. "The Formation of Learning Sets." *Psychological Review* 56 (1949): 51-65.

Harris, A. J.; Morrison, C.; Serwer, B. L.; and Gold, L. *A Continuation of CRAFT Project: Comparing Reading Approaches with Disadvantaged Urban Negro Children in Primary Grades.* New York: Division of Teacher Education of the City University of New York, 1968.

Haynes, H. C. "The Relation of Teacher Intelligence, Teacher Experience and Type of School to Types of Questions." Ph.D. dissertation, George Peabody College for Teachers, 1935.

Hecht, L. W. "Isolation From Learning Supports and the Processing of Group Instruction." Ph.D. dissertation, University of Chicago, 1977.

Hicklin, W. J. "A Study of Long-Range Techniques for Predicting Patterns of Scholastic Behavior." Ph.D. dissertation, University of Chicago, 1962.

Hiller, J. H. "Learning from Prose Text: Effects of Readability Level, Inserted Question Difficulty, and Individual Differences." *Journal of Educational Psychology* 66 (1974): 189-201.

Hops, H., and Cobb, J. A. *Survival Behaviors in the Educational Setting: Their Implications for Research and Intervention.* Eugene, Ore.: Department of Special Education, University of Oregon, 1972.

Hops, H., and Cobb, J. A. "Initial Investigations into Academic Survival—Skill Training, Direct Instruction, and First-Grade Achievement." *Journal of Educational Psychology* 66 (1974): 548-553.

Howe, M. J. A., and Colley, L. "The Influence of Questions Encountered Earlier on Learning from Prose." *British Journal of Educational Psychology* 46 (1976): 149-154.

Howe, M. J. A., and Singer, L. "Presentation Variables and Students' Activities in Meaningful Learning." *British Journal of Educational Psychology* 45 (1975): 52-61.

Hudgins, B. B. "Attending and Thinking in the Classroom." Symposium paper presented to the American Psychological Association Meeting, New York, 1966. (Mimeographed.)

Hughes, D. D. "An Experimental Investigation of the Effects of Pupil Responding and Teacher Reacting on Pupil Achievement. Experiment III: Teacher Reaction." *American Educational Research Journal* 1 (1973): 21-37.

Hunkins, F. P. "The Effects of Analysis and Evaluation Questions on Varying Levels of Achievement." Paper presented at the Annual Meeting of the American Educational Research Association, Chicago, 1968.

Hunkins, F. P. "The Influence of Analysis and Evaluation Questions on Achievement in Sixth Grade Social Studies." Paper presented at the Annual Meeting of the American Educational Research Association, New York, 1967.

Jackson, P. W. *Life in Classrooms.* New York: Holt, Rinehart and Winston, 1968.

Jackson, P. W., and Beford, E. "Educational Objectives and the Joys of Teaching." *School Review* 73 (1965): 267-291.

James, W. *Principles of Psychology, Vol. 1.* New York: Henry Holt and Company, 1890.

Johnson, D.; Johnson, R. T.; Johnson, J.; and Anderson, D. "Effects of Cooperative Versus Individualized Instruction on Students' Prosocial Behavior, Attitudes Toward Learning, and Achievement." *Journal of Educational Psychology* 68 (1976): 446-452.

Kaplan, R. "Effects of Grouping and Response Characteristics of Instructional Objectives on Learning from Prose." *Journal of Educational Psychology* 68 (1976): 424-430.

Kaplan, R., and Rothkopf, E. Z. "Instructional Objectives as Directions to Learners: Effects of Passage Length and Amount of Objective-Relevant Content." *Journal of Educational Psychology* 66 (1974): 448-456.

Kaplan, R., and Simmons, F. G. "Effects of Instructional Objectives Used as Orienting Stimuli or as Summary/Review Upon Prose Learning." *Journal of Educational Psychology* 66 (1974): 614-622.

Karabinus, R. A. "Differential Examination Feedback Treatments, Learning and Attitudes." Ph.D. dissertation, University of Illinois, 1966.

Karraker, R. J. "Knowledge of Results and Incorrect Recall of Plausible Multiple-Choice Alternatives." *Journal of Educational Psychology* 58 (1967): 11-14.

Kersh, M. E. "A Strategy for Mastery Learning in Fifth Grade Arithmetic." Ph.D. dissertation, University of Chicago, 1971.

Kim, Y.; Cho, G.; Park, J.; and Park, M. *An Application of a New Instructional Model (Research Report).* Seoul, Korea: Korean Educational Development Institute, 1974.

Klinger, R. L. *The Effects of Written, Positive Statements on Academic Performance of Fifth Grade Students.* Ph.D. dissertation, University of Texas at Austin, 1971.

Koran, M. L., and Koran, J. J., Jr. "Interaction of Learner Aptitudes with Question Pacing in Learning from Prose." *Journal of Educational Psychology* 67 (1975): 76-82.

Kounin, J. S., and Gump, P. F. "Signal Systems of Lesson Settings and the Task-Related Behavior of Preschool Children." *Journal of Educational Psychology* 66 (1974): 554-562.

Kownslar, A. O., ed. *Teaching American History.* Washington, D.C.: National Council for Social Studies Yearbook, 1974.

Krauskopf, C. J. "Use of Written Responses in the Stimulated Recall Method." *Journal of Educational Psychology* 54 (1963): 172-176.

Kulhavy, R. W.; Schmid, R. F.; and Walker, C. H. "Temporal Organization in Prose." *American Educational Research Journal* 14 (1977): 115-123.

Kulhavy, R. W., and Swenson, I. "Imagery Instructions and the Comprehension of Text." *British Journal of Educational Psychology* 45 (1975): 47-51.

Kulhavy, R. W.; Yekovich, F. R.; and Dyer, J. W. "Feedback and Response Confidence." *Journal of Educational Psychology* 68 (1976): 522-528.

Lahaderne, H. M. "Attitudinal and Intellectual Correlates of Attention: A Study of Four Classrooms." *Journal of Educational Psychology* 59 (1968): 320-324.

LaPorte, R. E., and Nath, R. "Role of Performance Goals in Prose Learning." *Journal of Educational Psychology* 68 (1976): 260-264.

Lawton, J. P. "Effects of Advance Organizer Lessons on Children's Use and Understanding of the Causal and Logical Because." Madison, Wisc.: University of Wisconsin, 1976. (Typewritten.)

Lawton, J. P., and Wanska, S. K. "Advance Organizers as a Teaching Strategy: A Reply to Barnes and Clawson." *Review of Educational Research* 47 (1977): 233-244.

Lee, S. S. "The Effects of Visually Represented Cues on Learning of Linear Function Rules." *Journal of Experimental Child Psychology* 12 (1971): 129-145.

Lee, S. S., and Dobson, L. N. "From Referents to Symbols: Visual Cues and Pointing Effects on Children's Acquisition of Linear Function Rules." *Journal of Educational Psychology* 69 (1977): 620-629.

Lesner, J. *The Effects of Pupil-Corrected Tests and Written Teacher Comments on Learning to Spell in the Upper Elementary Grades.* Ph.D. dissertation, University of California at Los Angeles, 1967.

Levin, J. R. "Inducing Comprehension in Poor Readers: A Test of a Recent Model." *Journal of Educational Psychology* 65 (1973): 19-24.

Levin, J. R.; Divine-Hawkins, P.; Kerst, S. M.; and Guttman, J. "Individual Differences in Learning from Pictures and Words: The Development and Application of an Instrument." *Journal of Educational Psychology* 66 (1974): 296-303.

Levin, T. "The Effect of Content Prerequisite and Process-Oriented Experiences on Application Ability in the Learning of Probability." Ph.D. dissertation, University of Chicago, 1975.

Levin, T. "Instruction Which Enables Students to Develop Higher Mental Processes." In *Evaluation in Education: An International Review Series.* Edited by B. H. Choppin and N. T. Postlesthwaite. Elmsford, N.Y.: Pergamon Press, 1979.

Levin T., and others. "Behavioral Patterns of Students Under an Individualized Learning Strategy." *Instructional Science* 9 (1980): 85-100.

Lloyd, K. E. "Contingency Management in University Courses." *Educational Technology* 11 (1971): 18-23.

Luchins, A. S., and Luchins, E. H. "New Experimental Attempts at Preventing Mechanisation in Problem Solving." *Journal of Genetic Psychology* 42 (1950); 279-297.

Mapel, S. B., Jr. *The Influence of the Instructor's Written Comments Upon Student Test Performance in the College Classroom.* Ph.D. dissertation, North Texas State University, 1970.

Marliave, R.; Fisher, C.; Fibby, N.; and Dishaw, M. "Beginning Teacher Evaluation Study." *Technical Reports 1-5: The Development of Instrumentation for a Field Study of Teaching.* Millerton, N.Y.: Far West Laboratory, 1977.

Marshall, W., and Mood, D. W. "Teacher Verbal Behavior and Teacher and Pupil Thinking in Elementary School." *The Journal of Educational Research* 66 (1972): 99-102.

May, M. A. "Enhancements and Simplifications of Stimulus Variables in A-V Presentations." A working paper. Washington, D.C.: U.S. Department of Health, Education and Welfare, 1965.

Mayer, R. E. "Different Problem Solving Competencies Established in Learning Computer Programming With and Without Meaningful Models." *Journal of Educational Psychology* 67 (1975): 725-734.

Mayer, R. E. "Forward Transfer of Different Reading Strategies Evoked by Test-Like Events in Mathematics Text." *Journal of Educational Psychology* 67 (1975): 165-169.

McConkie, G. W.; Rayner, K.; and Wilson, S. J. "Experimental Manipulation of Reading Strategies." *Journal of Educational Psychology* 65 (1973): 1-8.

McDonald, F. J. "Report on Phase II of Beginning Teacher Evaluation Study." *Journal of Teacher Education* 27 (1976): 39-42.

McGraw, B., and Grotelueschen, A. "Direction of the Effect of Questions in Prose Material." *Journal of Educational Psychology* 63 (1972): 580-588.

Measel, W., and Mood, D. W. "Teacher Verbal Behavior and Teacher and Pupil Thinking in Elementary School." *The Journal of Educational Research* 66 (1972): 99-102.

Melton, R. F. "Resolution of Conflicting Claims Concerning the Effect of Behavioral Objectives on Student Learning." *Review of Educational Research* 48 (1978): 291-302.

Miller, G. L. "Collaborative Teaching and Pupil Thinking." *Journal of Teacher Education* 17 (1966): 337-358.

Moody, F. E. *The Differential Effects of Teacher Comments on College Females' Achievement as Measured by Test Performance.* Ph.D. dissertation, University of Rochester, 1970.

Morsh, J. E. "Systematic Observations of Instructor Behavior." Developmental Report AFPTRC-TN-56-52. San Antonio, Tex.: Air Force Personnel and Training Research Center, Lackland Air Force Base, 1956.

Niedermeyer, F. C.; Brown, J.; and Sulzen, R. "Learning and Varying Sequences of Ninth-Grade Mathematics Materials." *Journal of Experimental Education* 37 (1969): 61-66.

Nuthall, G. "Improving Teaching Methods." In *Directions in New Zealand Secondary Education*. Edited by J. A. Codel. New York: The International P.U.B.N.S., 1976.

Olson, W. C. "A Study of Classroom Behavior." *Journal of Educational Psychology* 22 (1931): 449-454.

Özcelik, D. "Student Involvement in the Learning Process." Ph.D. dissertation, University of Chicago, 1973.

Packard, R. G. "The Control of 'Classroom Attention': A Group Contingency for Complex Behavior." *Journal of Applied Behavioral Analysis* 3 (1970): 13-28.

Page, E. B. "Teacher Comments and Student Performance: A Seventy-Four Classroom Experiment in School Motivation." *Journal of Educational Psychology* 49 (1958): 173-181.

Paivio, A. "Mental Imagery in Associative Learning and Memory." *Psychological Review* 76 (1969): 241-263.

Paivio, A. *Imagery and Verbal Processes*. New York: Holt, Rinehart and Winston, 1971.

Paradowski, W. "Effect of Curiosity on Incidental Learning." *Journal of Educational Psychology* 58 (1967): 50-55.

Payne, A. "The Selection and Treatment of Data for Certain Curriculum Decision Problems. A Methodological Study." Ph.D. dissertation, University of Chicago, 1963.

Perkins, H. V. "Classroom Behavior and Underachievement." *American Educational Research Journal* 2 (1965): 1-12.

Plowman, L., and Stroud, J. B. "Effect of Informing Pupils of the Correctness of Their Responses to Objective Test Questions." *Journal of Educational Research* 36 (1942): 16-20.

Reynolds, J. H., and Glaser, R. "Effects of Repetition and Spaced Review Upon Retention of a Complex Learning Task." *Journal of Educational Psychology* LV (1964): 297-308.

Rhoads, P. A. *Relationship Between Teacher Comments and the Performance of Slow Learners*. Ph.D. dissertation, University of Maryland, 1967.

Rice, D. R. "The Effect of Question-Asking Introduction on Preservice Elementary Science Teachers." *Journal of Research in Science Teaching* 14 (1977): 353-359.

Rickards, J. P., and August, G. J. "Generative Underlining Strategies in Prose Recall." *Journal of Educational Psychology* 67 (1975): 860-865.

Rickards, J. P., and DiVesta, F. J. "Type and Frequencies of Questions in Processing Textual Material." *Journal of Educational Psychology* 66 (1974): 354-362.

Rohwer, W. D., Jr., and Ammons, M. S. "Elaboration Training and Paired Associate Learning Efficiency in Children." *Journal of Educational Psychology* 62 (1971): 376-383.

Rohwer, W. D., Jr., and Harris, W. J. "Media Effects on Prose Learning in Two Populations of Children." *Journal of Educational Psychology* 67 (1975): 651-657.

Rohwer, W. D., Jr., and Matz, R. "Improving Aural Comprehension in White and Black Children. Pictures Versus Print." *Journal of Experimental Child Psychology* 19 (1975): 23-36.

Rosenshine, B. "Objectively Measured Behavioral Predictors of Effectiveness in Explaining." In *Research Into Classroom Processes, Recent Developments and Next Steps*. Edited by I. Westbury and A. A. Bellack. New York: Columbia University Teachers College Press, 1971a.

Rosenshine, B. *Teaching Behaviors and Student Achievement*. National Foundation for Educational Research in England and Wales, 1971b.

Rosenshine, B. "Classroom Instruction." In *The Psychology of Teaching Methods*. Edited by W. L. Gage. Chicago: University of Chicago Press, 1976.

Rosenshine, B. "Content, Time, and Direct Instruction." In *Research on Teaching: Concepts, Findings and Implications*. Edited by P. Peterson and H. Walberg. Berkeley, Cal.: McCutchan, 1979.

Ross, D. "Relationship Between Dependency, Intentional Learning and Incidental Learning in Preschool Children." *Journal of Personality and Social Psychology* 4 (1966): 374-381.

Rothkopf, E. Z. "Learning from Written Material: An Exploration of the Control of Inspection Behavior by Test-Like Events." *American Educational Research Journal* 3 (1966): 241-250.

Rothkopf, E.Z. "Variable Adjunct Question Schedules, Interpersonal Interaction and Incidental Learning from Written Material." *Journal of Educational Psychology* 63 (1972): 87-92.

Rothkopf, E. Z., and Bisbicos, E. E. "Selective Facilitative Effects of Interspersed Questions on Learning from Written Materials." *Journal of Educational Psychology* 58 (1967): 56-61.

Rothkopf, E. Z., and Kaplan, R. "Exploration of the Effect of Density and Specificity of Instructional Objectives on Learning from Text." *Journal of Educational Psychology* 63 (1972): 295-302.

Rothkopf, E. Z., and Koether, M. E. "Instructional Effects of Discrepancies in Content and Organization Between Study Goals and Information Sources." *Journal of Educational Psychology* 70 (1978): 67-71.

Royer, J. M., and Cable, G. W. "Illustrations, Analogies and Facilitative Transfer in Prose Learning." *Journal of Educational Psychology* 68 (1976): 205-209.

Royer, P. N. "Effects of Specificity and Position of Written Instructional Objectives on Learning from Lecture." *Journal of Educational Psychology* 69 (1977): 40-45.

Samuels, S. J., and Turnure, J. E. "Attention and Reading Achievement in First-Grade Boys and Girls." *Journal of Educational Psychology* 66 (1974): 29-32.

Sassenrath, J. M., and Garverick, C. M. "Effects of Differential Feedback from Examinations on Retention and Transfer." *Journal of Educational Psychology* 56 (1965): 259-263.

Scandura, J. M. "Expository Teaching of Hierarchical Subject Matter." *Journal of Structural Learning* 2 (1969): 17-25.

Schmidt, R. A. "A Schema Theory of Discrete Motor Skill Learning." *Psychological Review* 82 (1975): 225-260.

Schreiber, J. E. "Teachers' Question-Asking Techniques in Social Studies." Ph.D. dissertation, University of Iowa, 1967.

Sheppard, W. C., and MacDermot, H. G. "Design and Evaluation of a Programmed Course in Introductory Psychology." *Journal of Applied Behavior Analysis* 3 (1970): 5-11.

Shimron, J. "Imagery and the Comprehension of Prose by Elementary School Children." Ph.D. dissertation, University of Pittsburgh, 1974.

Shimron, J. "Learning Activities in Individually Prescribed Instruction." *Instructional Science* 5 (1976): 391-401.

Shrago, M. J. *The Effect of Approving Teacher Comments on Pupil Achievement and Attitude*. Ph.D. dissertation, University of Kansas, 1970.

Siegel, L.; Siegel, L. C.; Carpretta, P. J.; Jones, R. L.; and Berkowitz, H. "Students' Thoughts During Class: A Criterion of Educational Research." *Journal of Educational Psychology* 54 (1963): 45-61.

Simon, A., and Boyer, E. G., eds. *Mirrors for Behavior: An Anthology of Classroom Observation Instruments*. 14 volumes. Philadelphia: Research for Better Schools, 1967.

Simons, R. H. *The Effect of Written Differential Incentives on Academic Performance at the Upper Elementary Level.* Ph.D. dissertation, University of Miami, 1971.

Smith, J. K., and Wick, J. W. "Practical Problems of Attempting to Implement a Mastery Learning Program in a Large City School System." Paper presented to the Annual Meeting of the American Educational Research Association, 1976.

Smith, S. A. "The Effects of Two Variables on the Achievement of Slow Learners on a Unit in Mathematics." M.A. thesis, University of Maryland, 1967.

Soar, R. S. *An Integrative Approach to Classroom Learning.* Philadelphia: Temple University, 1966.

Solomon, D., and Kendall, A. J. *Final Report: Individual Characteristics and Children's Performance in Varied Educational Settings.* Spencer Foundation Project, 1976.

Spaulding, R. L. *Achievement, Creativity, and Self-Concept Correlates of Teacher-Pupil Transactions in Elementary Schools.* Hempstead, N.Y.: Hofstra University, 1965.

Spencer, R. E., and Barker, B. *An Applied Test of the Effectiveness of an Experimental Feedback Answer Sheet.* Research report 293. Urbana, Ill.: University of Illinois, Measurement and Research Division, Office of Instructional Resources, 1969.

Stallings, J. A. "How Instructional Processes Relate to Child Outcomes in a National Study of Follow Through." *Journal of Teacher Education* 27 (1976): 43-47.

Stallings, J. A. "The National Institute of Education Study of Teaching Basic Reading Skills in Secondary Schools." Paper presented at the Annual Meeting of the American Educational Research Association, 1978.

Stallings, J. A., and Kaskowitz, D. *Follow-Through Classroom Observation Evaluation, 1972-73* Menlo Park, Cal.: Stanford Research Institute, 1974.

Starkey, K. T. *The Effect of Teacher Comments on Attitude Toward and Achievement in Secondary Mathematics Classes: An Experimental Study.* Ph.D. dissertation, Pennsylvania State University, 1971.

Steg, D.; Mattleman, M.; and Hammill, D. "Effects of Individual Programmed Instruction on Initial Reading Skills and Language Behavior in Early Childhood." Paper presented to the International Reading Association, Boston, 1968.

Stevens, R. "The Question as a Measure of Efficiency in Instruction: A Critical Study of Classroom Practice." *Teachers College Contributions to Education* 48 (1912).

Stewart, L. G., and White, M. A. "Teacher Comments, Letter Grades, and Student Performance: What Do We Really Know?" *Journal of Educational Psychology* 68 (1976): 488-500.

Sturges, P. T. "Effects of Instruction and Form of Informative Feedback on Retention of Meaningful Material." *Journal of Educational Psychology* 63 (1972b): 99-102.

Sturges, P. T. "Information Delay and Retention: Effect of Information in Feedback and Tests." *Journal of Educational Psychology* 63 (1972a): 32-43.

Sturges, P. T. "Verbal Retention as a Function of the Informativeness and Delay of Informative Feedback." *Journal of Educational Psychology* 60 (1969): 11-14.

Surber, J. R., and Anderson, R. C. "Delay-Retention Effect in Natural Classroom Settings." *Journal of Educational Psychology* 67 (1975): 170-173.

Sweet, R. C. *Educational Attainment and Attitudes Toward School as a Function of Feedback in the Form of Teachers' Written Comments.* Madison, Wisc.: University of Wisconsin, 1966. (ERIC Document Reproduction Service No. ED 015 163.)

Taba, H.; Levine, S.; and Elzey, F. F. *Thinking in Elementary School Children.* San Francisco: State College, 1964.

Tenenbaum, A. B. "Task-Dependent Effects of Organization and Context Upon Comprehension of Prose." *Journal of Educational Psychology* 69 (1977): 528-536.

Tenenberg, M. S. "Effects of Different Study Instructions on Learning from Written Materials." Ph.D. dissertation, University of California at Berkeley, 1969.

Thorndike, E. L. *Human Learning*. New York: Century, 1931.

Tinsley, D. C.; Watson, E. P.; and Marshall, J. C. "Cognitive Objectives Revealed by Classroom Questions on Process-Oriented and Context-Oriented Secondary Social Studies Programs." Paper presented at the Annual Meeting of the American Educational Research Association, Minneapolis, 1970.

Traub, R. E. "Importance of Problem Heterogeneity to Programmed Instruction." *Journal of Educational Psychology* 57 (1966): 54-60.

Travers, R. M. W., ed. *Second Handbook of Research on Teaching*. Chicago: Rand McNally, 1973.

Travers, R. M. W.; Van Wagenen, R. K.; Haygood, D. H.; and McCormick, M. "Learning as a Consequence of the Learner's Task Involvement Under Different Conditions of Feedback." *Journal of Educational Psychology* 55 (1964).

Tulving, E. "Cue-Dependent Forgetting." *American Scientist* 62 (1974): 74-82.

Turnure, J. E., and Samuels, S. J. *Attention and Reading Achievement in First Grade Boys and Girls*. Research Report No. 43. St. Paul, Minn.: University of Minnesota Research Development and Demonstration Center in Education of Handicapped Children, 1972.

Tyler, R. W. *Basic Principles of Curriculum and Instruction*. Chicago: University of Chicago Press, 1949.

Van Wagenen, R. K., and Travers, R. M. W. "Learning Under Conditions of Direct and Vicarious Reinforcement." *Journal of Educational Psychology* 54 (1963): 356-362.

Vohs, J. L. "An Empirical Approach to the Concept of Attention." *Speech Monographs* 31 (1964): 355-360.

Walker, H. M.; Mattson, R. H.; and Buckley, N. K. "Special Class Placement as a Treatment Alternative for Deviant Behavior in Children." In *Modifying Deviant Social Behaviors in Various Classroom Settings*. Edited by F. A. M. Benson. Monograph No. 1. Eugene, Ore.: University of Oregon, Department of Special Education, 1969.

Watts, G. H., and Anderson, R. C. "Effects of Three Types of Inserted Questions on Learning from Written Materials." *Journal of Educational Psychology* 62 (1971): 387-394.

Wentling, T. L. "Mastery Versus Nonmastery Instruction with Varying Test Item Feedback Treatments." *Journal of Educational Psychology* 65 (1973): 50-58.

Wesley, F. "Silents, Please." *Audio-Visual Communications Review* 10 (1962): 102-105.

Wheeler, R., and Ryan, F. "Effects of Cooperative and Competitive Classroom Environments on the Attitudes and Achievement of Elementary School Students Engaged in Social Studies Inquiry Activities." *Journal of Educational Psychology* 65 (1973): 402-407.

Williams, R. L. "Relationship of Class Participation to Personality, Ability, Achievement Variables." *Journal of Social Psychology* 83 (1971): 193-198.

Wilson, J. H. "The New Science Teachers are Asking More and Better Questions." *Journal of Research in Science Teaching* 6 (1969): 303-308.

Wittrock, M. C. "The Evaluation of Instruction: Cause-and-Effect Relations in Naturalistic Data." In *The Evaluation of Instruction: Issues and Problems*. Edited by M. C. Wittrock and D. E. Wiley. New York: Holt, Rinehart and Winston, Inc., 1970.

Wright, C. J., and Nuthall, G. "Relationships Between Teacher Behaviors and Pupil Achievement in Three Elementary Science Lessons." *American Educational Research Journal* 7 (1970): 477-493.

Yoloye, A. E. "Observational Techniques." In *Handbook of Curriculum Evaluation*. Edited by A. Lewy. New York: Longman, Inc., 1977.

Zahorik, J. A. "Classroom Feedback Behavior of Teachers." *The Journal of Educational Research* 62 (1968): 147-150.

Zeaman, D., and House, B. J. "The Relation of IQ and Learning." In *Learning and Individual Differences.* Edited by R. Gagne. Columbus, Oh.: C.E. Merrill Books, 1967.

Zeaman, D., and House, B. J. "The Role of Attention in Retardate Discrimination Learning." In *Handbook of Mental Deficiency.* Edited by N. R. Ellis. New York: McGraw-Hill, 1963.

About the Authors

TAMAR LEVIN is on the faculty of the School of Education, Tel Aviv University, Tel Aviv, Israel.

RUTH LONG is Associate Director for the Association for Supervision and Curriculum Development, Alexandria, Virginia.

ASCD Publications, Spring 1981

Yearbooks

A New Look at Progressive Education
(610-17812) $8.00
Considered Action for Curriculum Improvement
(610-80186) $9.75
Education for an Open Society
(610-74012) $8.00
Evaluation as Feedback and Guide
(610-17700) $6.50
Feeling, Valuing, and the Art of Growing:
Insights into the Affective
(610-77104) $9.75
Life Skills in School and Society
(610-17786) $5.50
Lifelong Learning—A Human Agenda
(610-79160) $9.75
Perceiving, Behaving, Becoming: A New Focus
for Education (610-17278) $5.00
Perspectives on Curriculum Development
1776-1976 (610-76078) $9.50
Schools in Search of Meaning
(610-75044) $8.50
Staff Development/Organization Development
(610-81232) $9.75

Books and Booklets

About Learning Materials (611-78134) $4.50
Action Learning: Student Community Service
Projects (611-74018) $2.50
Adventuring, Mastering, Associating: New
Strategies for Teaching Children
(611-76080) $5.00
Approaches to Individualized Education
(611-80204) $4.75
Bilingual Education for Latinos
(611-78142) $6.75
Classroom-Relevant Research in the Language
Arts (611-78140) $7.50
Clinical Supervision—A State of the Art Review
(611-80194) $3.75
Curricular Concerns in a Revolutionary Era
(611-17852) $6.00
Curriculum Leaders: Improving Their Influence
(611-76084) $4.00
Curriculum Materials 1980 (611-80198) $3.00
Curriculum Theory (611-77112) $7.00
Degrading the Grading Myths: A Primer of
Alternatives to Grades and Marks
(611-76082) $6.00
Educating English-Speaking Hispanics
(611-80202) $6.50
Elementary School Mathematics: A Guide to
Current Research (611-75056) $5.00
Eliminating Ethnic Bias in Instructional
Materials: Comment and Bibliography
(611-74020) $3.25
Global Studies: Problems and Promises for
Elementary Teachers (611-76086) $4.50
Handbook of Basic Citizenship Competencies
(611-80196) $4.75
Humanistic Education: Objectives and
Assessment (611-78136) $4.75
Learning More About Learning
(611-17310) $2.00
Measuring and Attaining the Goals of Education
(611-80210) $6.50

Middle School in the Making
(611-74024) $5.00
The Middle School We Need
(611-75060) $2.50
Moving Toward Self-Directed Learning
(611-79166) $4.75
Multicultural Education: Commitments, Issues,
and Applications (611-77108) $7.00
Needs Assessment: A Focus for Curriculum
Development (611-75048) $4.00
Observational Methods in the Classroom
(611-17948) $3.50
Open Education: Critique and Assessment
(611-75054) $4.75
Partners: Parents and Schools
(611-79168) $4.75
Professional Supervision for Professional
Teachers (611-75046) $4.50
Reschooling Society: A Conceptual Model
(611-17950) $2.00
The School of the Future—NOW
(611-17920) $3.75
Schools Become Accountable: A PACT
Approach (611-74016) $3.50
The School's Role as Moral Authority
(611-77110) $4.50
Selecting Learning Experiences: Linking
Theory and Practice (611-78138) $4.75
Social Studies for the Evolving Individual
(611-17952) $3.00
Staff Development: Staff Liberation
(611-77106) $6.50
Supervision: Emerging Profession
(611-17796) $5.00
Supervision in a New Key (611-17926) $2.50
Urban Education: The City as a Living
Curriculum (611-80206) $6.50
What Are the Sources of the Curriculum?
(611-17522) $1.50
Vitalizing the High School (611-74026) $3.50
Developmental Characteristics of Children and
Youth (wall chart) (611-75058) $2.00

Discounts on quantity orders of same title to
single address: 10-49 copies, 10%; 50 or more
copies, 15%. Make checks or money orders
payable to ASCD. Orders totaling $20.00 or
less must be prepaid. Orders from institutions
and businesses must be on official purchase
order form. Shipping and handling charges will
be added to billed purchase orders. *Please be
sure to list the stock number of each publica-
tion, shown in parentheses.*

Subscription to *Educational Leadership*—$18.00
a year. ASCD Membership dues: Regular (subscription [$18] and yearbook)—$34.00 a year;
Comprehensive (includes subscription [$18]
and yearbook plus other books and booklets
distributed during period of membership)—
$44.00 a year.

Order from:

**Association for Supervision and
Curriculum Development
225 North Washington Street
Alexandria, Virginia 22314**